Rusting Tin **&** Shiny Plastic

From Elm Park to the Madejski Stadium – the story of a football cultural revolution

Zac Josey   Roger Titford

Further Thought Publishing in association with Zac Josey

1999

Images copyright Zac Josey

Text copyright Roger Titford

First published in Great Britain in 1999 by

Further Thought Publishing in association with Zac Josey

High Griff House

Heads Lane

Inkpen, Berks RG17 9QS

A CIP CATALOGUE RECORD FOR THIS BOOK IS AVAILABLE FROM THE BRITISH LIBRARY

ISBN 0-9518771 1 9

Designed by Zac Josey

Map on page 12 drawn by Peter Cook of The Whiff.

Cover designed by John Ball at Cartwheel, Swindon.

Printed and bound in Great Britain by Fairway Press, Reading

FOR RAY JOSEY

1922- 1986

FOR HOLLY

Who had one sniff
of the old ways –
welcome to the new

FOR READING FANS

Elm Park.

ACKNOWLEDGEMENTS

On a formal level we would like to acknowledge permissions received to reproduce written or photographic material copyright of Harry Pearson, Gerard Gadney (p30), the Reading Evening Post, David Downs, Harold Hill (p28), the Whiff fanzine and Rural History Department at Reading University (p22).

We would also like to thank the following for providing help, information or comment: Fred Neate, Frank Orton, Alan Sedunary, Haydn Middleton, Ben Sharpe, Nigel Howe, Colin Bishop's video collection, Steve at CPL (Reading), John Ball at Cartwheel (Swindon), Brett King (computer wizard), David Pitson, Anna Glanville-Smith at Reading College, James Spettigue, Chris Leah, Duncan Longdon, Pete at the Whiff, Graham Loader, Paul at Fairway Press. Also for their support we thank Dorothy Newman, Penny and Bob Warren, Chris and Carol Josey, Christine and Cecil King and, especially, Zoe and Christine.

We would also like to wish well those kind enough to write forewords to this book and those who have subscribed to this book. Your names, hopefully, appear on pages 246 and 247.

FOREWORDS

We all here at Reading Football Club are very grateful to Zac for this wonderful photographic essay showing the dramatic move from Elm Park to the new stadium.

His work is very evocative and captures succinctly the mood, reality and atmosphere of both these very special occasions. I am sure many people will be moved as they turn the pages of this poignant photographic and historical document. It is even more poignant as it is difficult to imagine that we will be moving to a new stadium again during any of our lifetimes.

I hope this book will also motivate more people to come and visit our lovely stadium and join with us in inspiring Reading to conquer the very pinnacles of success in football.

John Madejski

It gives me great pleasure to be asked to write a brief foreword for this book, which has documented one of the biggest changes myself and you fans have seen.

After playing at a stadium for so long one gets to know it as a friend. Elm Park was one of the finest grounds to play at, in terms of its atmosphere. The fact that the players and the fans were so close together created a unity for the team. It gave me a chance to play in a place that cared passionately for football and showed it as well.

My favourite memory of Elm Park will stay with me forever. It was the game against Brighton in 1994 where we finally clinched the Division Two Championship with one match to spare. The feeling of hearing that final whistle and seeing the crowd surging on to the pitch was fantastic and one that will always endear me to Elm Park.

The move to the Madejski Stadium was huge on all levels. From my point of view the facilities are second to none and perfect for producing top quality football. Even with crowds of 10,000 the atmosphere is still good and it is only a matter of time before we start showing the class I know we are capable of. Unfortunately during the timespan of this book the football has not been of top quality but I am sure this will change dramatically very soon.

Phil Parkinson

I enjoyed my time at Elm Park and am still enjoying my time at the Madejski Stadium. The game has changed enormously since I joined Reading as a player in 1956. Then we had more local boys playing for the team, staying at the club for a long time and playing for the love of the game.

There was no sponsorship of players' boots. We used to choose our own from Blake's Sports shop, nail the studs into the soles and top them up with leather. The pitches used to get very heavy in the winter months and so did the ball and the boots! With better drainage and water systems and less use the pitches are much better today. Mind you, very few games got postponed at Elm Park.

The facilities there were not so good but at the Madejski Stadium they are excellent and the floodlights are nearly as good as daylight.

Gordon 'Fred' Neate

My experiences of Elm Park started at a very early age when my mum took me along to watch my dad (Douggie) play but my memory of those days is a bit hazy. Growing up I stood on the Tilehurst End watching my team play every home game. I always wanted to start my career at Reading and my wish came true when I made my full debut for my home-town team at the age of 16.

As a fan, the memories that stand out are when Reading played Arsenal in the FA Cup in 1972 and scored all three goals but still managed to lose 1-2! And, of course, of watching Robin Friday play and seeing him score probably the best goal I have ever seen, with referee Clive Thomas applauding the feat. As a player I recall making my home debut in a 1-1 draw against Rotherham and scoring my first goal at Elm Park against Swindon. I still have a framed photo of that.

The difference between Elm Park and the Madejski Stadium is unbelievable. You could not ask for two more different stadia but Elm Park, for all its faults, still holds great memories. The club is now geared for a tremendous future and hopefully, with the facilities we now have, Premiership football in the foreseeable future is, with any luck, not out of the question.

Neil Webb

As I was only based at Elm Park for a few games I haven't got the memories and experiences that many of you have. However, I cannot forget my first visit to Elm Park. It was the game before I had agreed to become manager of Reading. We were playing Huddersfield and I had come down to see what the fan base was like and get a sense of the overall atmosphere of the club. Stood at the back of the South Bank in amongst all the fans was quite an experience. The passion and emotion that emanated from there was incredible. The singing and style of support showed me this was a hotbed and within 45 minutes I knew this was the type of support that would entice me to the club. With support like that you feel you have a moral victory already.

Unfortunately after losing at Nottingham Forest and getting relegated, the final game against Norwich was a real anti-climax. It would have been good to leave Elm Park on a high. The place would have left people with a lot of very special memories.

The experience of going to a game at Elm Park was very old-fashioned, a couple of drinks beforehand and an entertaining atmosphere. The Madejski Stadium is a dramatically different culture what with the corporate hospitality and the all-seater stadium. This creates a slightly muted atmosphere but I firmly believe this will change.

Tommy Burns

The Madejski Stadium.

Rusting Tin & Shiny Plastic came about through the merger of two different strands of work. Back in 1993, when Reading's move from Elm Park was still not decided upon, I started work on writing what was intended to be a 'centenary history' of Elm Park due for publication in 1996. When it became clear that the Madejski Stadium was going to be built the 'centenary history' idea rather faded away. Why write a 100 year history when you know the story is going to last exactly 102 years? Family, business and my Supporters' Club commitments all told against completing the book as originally envisaged though sections of it have crept out into the club programme and the Evening Post and some of the interviews and old photos collected are used here.

In the meantime, inspired by a course on design and a keen interest in football, Zac Josey had begun collecting his photographic record of the last years of Elm Park. One day early in the first season at the Madejski Stadium he stopped me and said. "Here, are you Roger Titford? I'd like you to do the writing in a book I'm producing." Fair enough, I thought.

It was Zac's concept to take a 'last season/first season' approach and that approach inevitably gave rise to comparing the experiences of fans in both arenas. Such was the material difference between the two stadia we thought we would reflect it directly in the title, picking out an element that encapsulates each age. Several clubs have moved grounds in recent years but none so suddenly and dramatically as Reading. The new stadium in itself was a mission statement for the club, saying that the lower division days should now be over. The move offered as complete a revolution in football culture as has ever been offered to one set of fans.

This book is, in effect, a self-publishing venture, done more because we feel it ought to be done and could be done. Many that Zac spoke to thought it could not be done. If there's any lesson to be had then it is that determination and mutual respect amongst those with a true sporting or friendly nature can still get you a long way. It's not all about power and money yet.

Our story, in images and words is, of course, a personal one. We recognise our views may, at times, be in the minority and acknowledge that where appropriate in the text. There is a little more on Elm Park than the Madejski Stadium but it is, after all, 102 times older at the point of writing! The story there is much fuller and now complete. Rusting Tin & Shiny Plastic seeks to recognise, and pay tribute to, the part it played in our footballing lives. But it can only reveal the first chapter of our new lives, only begin to say how they are different and only hint at the story to come.

CONTENTS

RUSTING TIN

CONTENTS

SHINY PLASTIC

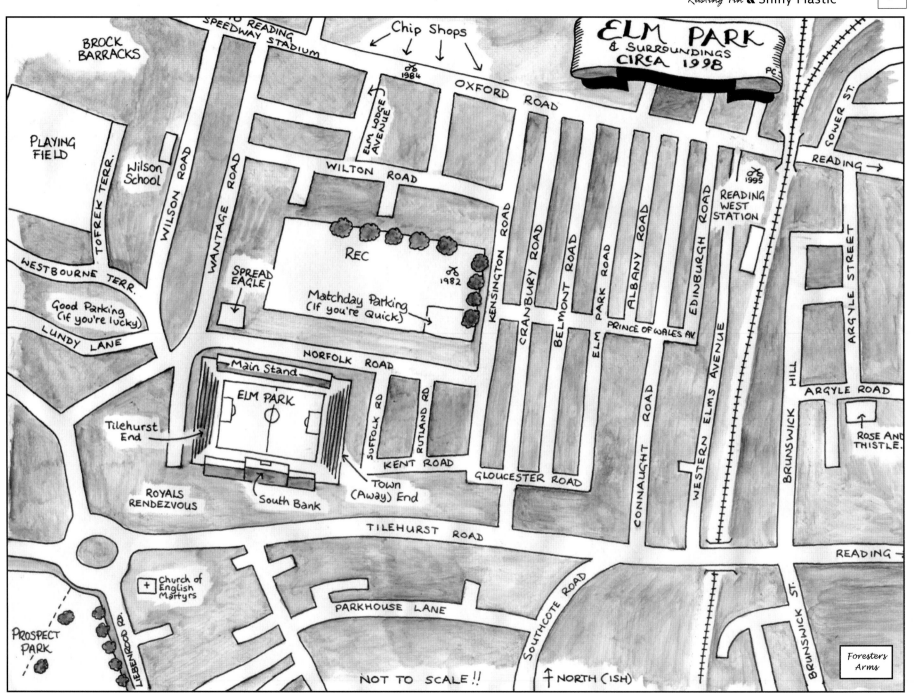

PART ONE   **ALL ABOUT ELM PARK**

From Where I Stood

It took a long, long time to realise quite what Elm Park meant to me. Then one December lunchtime in the mid-1980s I was sat with a pre-match pint in the front bar of the Foresters in Brunswick Street. Outside it was back-street grey and drizzly, inside there was the familiar warm hubbub of greetings, football talk and drink ordering. I was sat waiting at a cheap copper-topped table, replete with plastic ash-tray, crisp packets and beer glass rings. My mate was late, but he was coming from Japan.

I was just back from Finland so it was a big effort all round to get back for this one and we were both knackered. Knackered with stilted meetings, business cards, running orders, overhead projectors, airports and all the stuff of business adulthood. We could have stayed where we each were for the weekend but we would rather have a decent pint and the prospect of becoming our real, simple selves again for the afternoon. Get into that dark cave of the South Bank, surround yourself with your unknown fellows to keep the wind out, and just stand, shout and cheer like you were 10 years old again. The complexities of life reduced down to just win, draw or lose. Let Martin Hicks do the worrying for an hour and a half!

It was a homing instinct, it was what I would rather do than anything at that moment and I wouldn't have made the flight back for an away game. It was a connection not just to do with football but also with childhood and growing up, with continuity and community. Follow a football club long enough and it becomes a mirror to your past. You change, society changes but the essence of football does not: we still have to beat Bournemouth and get out of the 'third' division! You can measure yourself growing up, and old, against the same constant spectacle from the same viewpoint in the ground. My place for over a quarter of a century was at the back of the South Bank on the halfway line, the roof coming down low and obscuring the sky so it was like peering at football through a large letterbox.

Elm Park was, in a sense, one of my homes and I wanted to see exactly what went on there. For those in middle age and above, your football ground may be the only place you have known well as both adult and child, one of the few places where you have run almost the whole gamut of emotions: from joy, pride, exhilaration and delight to shock, rage, boredom, fear and disappointment. The football ground was an irreplaceable anchor in many lives. Writer Harry Pearson suggested, "people who don't follow football think of it as just a game, something that can be packed away when it is finished and forgotten about. But the game, played out by 22 men in an hour and a half, is only the kernel of something greater.

The mouth of the cave.

The game is the core, you might say of the Game... People wound strands of their everyday life around it – childhood, youth, work, friendships, relatives, experiences, memories – until football became inextricable from existence itself." Whenever I rejoined the geographic centre of that existence by turning up and into the Tilehurst Road there was always a slight physical reaction; my stride quickened. Or as the car entered Liebenrood Road, the foot came down a little too far on the accelerator. Every nearby street corner held some kind of memory.

And inside the turnstiles this sense of continuity was compounded by the unchanging nature of Elm Park. I can think of no ground, and I've been to them all, that has had changed less over the last 40 years than Elm Park. Like an elderly relative's front room, it was a place you could come back to and expect to be much as you left it a fortnight ago. At the start of each season there would be a fear of something unasked for, an irrelevant improvement made over the summer. But, from the day I first went there in 1964 to the day it closed, it remained, to the spectator's eye, basically unchanged; the same two covered sides – one seated one not, the same two uncovered ends.

I was born in Battle Hospital and spent my impressionable childhood years at Wilson Road school, respectively one- and two-and-a-half goal-kicks away (as these things are traditionally measured) from Elm Park. My family home for over 40 years was a 10 minute walk away and our back garden seemed to be on the same contour line of the valley of the Thames as the Elm Park pitch, a kind of geographical umbilical chord connecting these two homes. When he was working in the garden my dad used to 'keep the score' by counting the unmistakeable roars for a home goal.

Often the most devoted adherents are born, bred and live closest to the shrine. David Downs, the Reading FC historian and myself both went to Wilson Road school, although years apart. Coincidence? No, the most influential teacher there, Mrs Barnes, was for many years a C Stand season ticket holder. Zac Josey, too, went to school there many years later and lived less than a goal-kick from the ground.

Over my Elm Park years, the 34 of them, I estimate I watched between 800 and 1000 games, including reserves, friendlies and all the other stuff; almost certainly twice as many as any player would ever have played in. Think of those hours spent, then double them to include the travel time getting there. It comes to the equivalent of investing two years of your working life! Some old supporters can probably treble my tally. I have seen games from all four sides of the ground, up high or down low, from the Directors Box and the PA booth, in blizzards and baking sunshine and games abandoned by fog or flood.

Through the letterbox.

I have made my own small marks on the place. The Golden Gate, where you could pay a £1 extra to get in quicker and have a chance of winning a prize draw, was my idea. So, too, from my marketing professional existence was the name 'Network SouthEast' which came back to haunt me when that part of British Rail sponsored the signage on the South Bank. Could have been worse, could have been someone else's effort like 'City, Coast and Country' enclosure!

Growing up near a professional football ground may have given my friends and me a sharper appreciation of Reading's place in football's 'ladder of life'. There was a connectedness that we could see between our own games in Prospect Park as kids and the local teams playing there at weekends; between local players taken on trial by the club and the Reading players training in the park during the week; between our own schoolboy dreams and the only place in town from where a real football result was announced to the nation. The better of us, and we knew no better players then, could expect to be taken on by the major clubs in just a few years! Our staple reading material was Football Monthly, always replete with stories of stars found in most unlikely circumstances and comics like Hotspur and Valiant full of soccer heroes with improbable backgrounds. And to show it wasn't all pie-in-the-sky we saw, in time, Steve Wicks graduate from our Wilson Road playground to a career at Chelsea, Derby and QPR.

Elm Park played its part in football's 'ladder of life', hosting, always 'by kind permission of the Directors', schools matches and local league Cup Finals. In the days before regular away travel and live TV coverage Elm Park was almost our entire football context as well as at the end of our road. Every now and again the stars of faraway football galaxies, men important enough to be featured on chewing gum cards and in football annuals, might alight on our turf and that was so important to us as football fans. We wanted to see these men down our road, to connect us as fans via them to the summits of the game they had experienced. We wanted Cantona in our yard, to see him in our childhood 'home' in back-street, humdrum Reading, to put him alongside our other Elm Park memories, to see whether he could score at the same end that Bobby Charlton did and to say 'I was there' – the match-goer's ultimate justification.

And more than just this, this bringing the magic of the game into your very own streets, Elm Park came to have for me a social dimension. As an informal, accessible venue it was the foundation of casually and gradually acquired friendships – "See you in the usual place" – or just find who else turned up on the day, no prior arrangement necessary. Some were sup-porters I only knew because of where they stood and if they were not there the bond was broken unless or until coincidence restored it.

To the match.

What brought them back time and again was not the ties of a real geographic community but a community that exists within our own imaginations, a re-creation of an idealised past or perhaps, just, a chance to have a beer with some old mates. A 'home' match in this context doesn't just mean the opposite of 'away'. It _is_ a kind of home. It doesn't move away. You always expect it to be open for you on match day.

To live in this way, to 'own' in your mind a place like this for the duration of your life, is a luxury not a right. Only the nobility in their stately homes are able to think differently. Elm Park has died because the blow of the Hillsborough disaster, on top of 40 years of inertia, meant too much change for the place to bear. Regrets? A whole bundle. Arguments? None really.

The greater entity is the club, the shirt and the shared memory of all its fans. The club outlives its individual supporters. Its continuing existence is a partnership between the dead, the living and the yet-to-be-born. The dead have done all they can in forming and nurturing the club. Now the living must protect and strengthen it both for themselves and the generations of Reading supporters still to come. By all conventional, rational judgements, if Reading Football Club had stayed at Elm Park, it would be handing down a weak and paltry inheritance. By moving, the club can be renewed after a century of, be honest, comparative failure. Of course, it hurts for some of us – and it does not for others less closely tied - but there's no argument about the rightness of the basic fact of the matter. However, it means a way of football life is over. We have lost forever a large part of that mirror on ourselves that is football and the simple, comforting, mundane shabbiness of an old home. And, no doubt, the front bar of the Foresters is carpeted now!

At this particular moment in time (summer 1999) Elm Park basks in rosy hindsight while the Madejski Stadium is yet to be seen in its best light. In 15 years time, when most of the crowd will never have stood at a football match, the Elm Park experience might look as appetising as a cock-fighting contest in a pub yard does to us today. But there was a time when that was OK too. On the following pages we aim to record in images and words what we Reading fans have so suddenly lost and gained.

Have a beer in the Rendezvous.

Meet your mates on the South Bank.

Kensington Road, not long after Elm Park opened.

The Move To Elm Park

Berkshire and the Thames Valley was a football 'hotbed' years before the game ever took off in Manchester, Liverpool or the North East! Reading, founded in 1871, are the oldest League club in the south of England. Nearby Marlow are the only club to have entered the FA Cup every season and they played Maidenhead in the very first FA Cup tie in 1871/2. Each of the next five finals were contested by at least one club with strong Thames Valley connections: Old Etonians or Oxford University. Reading themselves entered the tournament in 1877/8, which gives us the dubious distinction of having lost more FA Cup-ties than any other League club! The Second Round draw (effectively the last 32) for 1881/2 shows, besides Maidenhead, Marlow and Old Etonians, *three* sides from Reading (Abbey and Minster being the other two), but only one from Liverpool and none at all from Manchester or the North East.

All this was to change by the end of the decade with the advent of professionalism in the North of England. The Football League was founded in April 1888 and its first, short-lived competitor emerged within a fortnight. By 1892 the Football Alliance had become the Second Division of the Football League. In 1893 Woolwich Arsenal were the first Southern club to join the League, leaving Millwall, the only other professional team in the South, without a league to play in. Professional football, organised on a league system, was now in great public demand.

Reading, still amateurs playing just over the Thames in Caversham, had an interesting 1893/4 season. In the FA Cup we beat Southampton and Swindon in the qualifying rounds to reach the last 32 and a tie at Deepdale. Five years previously Preston were famously the Invincibles; now they were in relegation trouble but they still beat us 18-0 to emphasise the gap that professionalism had opened up. In the FA Amateur Cup we also made progress to the Quarter Final before losing to Old Carthusians in front of a crowd of 1,000, many of whom had braved a trip across the February Thames on a punt. Besides the extra expense, a whole old penny, the difficulties of access must have served as a deterrent to frail and the impatient. Plus ca change as one might say 104 years later.

Despite retaining their amateur status Reading joined a number of professional clubs in forming the Southern League in 1894/5. We finished in mid-table in a league dominated by the professionals. Public interest and the demand for competitive success was driving the club to embrace professionalism, though the old guard of the amateur days, represented by founding President James Simonds (of the Reading brewing family), opposed it and subsequently resigned.

"It was on 27th May 1895 that F.A.Cox, a former chairman, moved the resolution that Reading should become a professional club and was supported by a big majority. With a semi-professional team attracting attention, the next thing that had to be considered was fresh headquarters. Prior to 1895 the club played at Caversham which was reached by ferry punts across the river. Boatmen had special instructions to exercise caution as Reading could ill-afford to lose a punt-load of supporters in those days," Athletic News wrote in 1930.

The site the club chose, in preference to Palmer Park or land behind the Moderation pub on the Reading side of Caversham Bridge, was in the west of the town on the edge of the Parliamentary boundary. It was effectively a 19th century greenfield site, out by the Workhouse and the Fever Hospital. An 1877 map shows just one large villa in the whole area between what is today Oxford Road, Wilson Road, Tilehurst Road and Elm Park Road, where now literally thousands live. That villa was called Elm Lodge and it still stands today, wedged into Wilton Road, and is an old people's home. When the property was auctioned in 1867 it was described as having pleasure gardens, an 18 acre park and a 58 acre farm. It was acquired by sports enthusiast, Councillor Jesse, in 1888. My 'educated' guess is that part of the farmland had been used for a few years as a gravel pit and brick works and this was the 4 acres that the Councillor leased to the Football Club on generous terms. Nearby Berkshire County Cricket Club had just been established on adjacent land at Kensington Road that in 1919 was bought by Huntley & Palmers FC and is now a recreation ground.

According to Alan Sedunary there is a record of Reading FC playing the Grenadier Guards at 'Elm Park' in November 1894 when the Caversham ground was flooded but it is thought this took place on the cricket ground to the north rather than the as yet undeveloped football ground site.

When Reading moved to Elm Park 'proper', Wantage Road and Norfolk Road were uninhabited, except for the Spread Eagle on the corner, and Tilehurst Road was little more than a country lane. But development was fast and within 15 years the surrounding terraced streets were much as we know them today. The houses were for ordinary working families. Improving activities were encouraged through several churches, two schools and a local library and the Spread Eagle continued to stand alone as the only pub in the quadrant.

The name 'Elm Park' was used on the opening match poster and presumably naturally flowed from the proximity to Elm Lodge.

The opening match, a friendly against A. Roston Bourke's London XI on 5th September 1896, was a public relations embarrassment of epic proportions. Mr Murdoch, with all the credibility a local Member of Parliament can muster, opened the ground with the words that "it is second to none in the kingdom". Then, in a thunderstorm, play commenced and was later abandoned, with Reading leading 7-1, in order to prevent further damage to the pitch and the turf terraces. A crowd of 2,500 went home early and the club was subsequently fined by the Football Association for playing unregistered opponents.

The Elm Park era had begun and continued in flamboyant fashion with an 8-3 win over Royal Ordnance a week later. Millwall were the first opponents to win at Elm Park in our third home League fixture but defeats were rare. Elm Park soon became a fortress with a record of played 47, won 33, drawn 8, lost 6, over the first 4 seasons. At the turn of the century, Reading would almost certainly be counted among the top 40 clubs in the country. Football League First Division opponents were matched or beaten in the FA Cup which, but for the dishonourable play of fellow Southern Leaguers Tottenham in the Quarter Final, we might even have won in 1901! Football boomed in the Edwardian era as entrepreneurs sought to make money from the professional game. Teams with no previous playing pedigree at all, like Chelsea and Bradford City, were simply invented and inserted into the Football League.

Connection to the railway network, particularly in Chelsea's case, was often an important factor in ground development. In May 1908 Reading were presented with an opportunity to develop the site opposite Reading General station, called Flanagan's Meadow between where the Mecca and Foster Wheeler now stand. But, Great Western Railways apart, the club appeared to have no influential supporters in the town and the scheme fell to protests by local residents and traders. Councillor Jackson said the move would be "a great curse to the town ...the better class of people who are in the habit of coming to Reading would cease coming if they are met by the crowd outside the station". Had it gone ahead, it might have forced Reading to adopt a more ambitious stance towards getting Football League membership. Tottenham and Fulham did leave the Southern League around this time and consequently enjoyed a 'headstart' over their former rivals that lasted many decades. Reading, more timid or less prosperous or both, simply waited with the rest of the Southern League to be absorbed as Division Three in 1920. By then the club had decided to settle in and develop Elm Park.

Elm Park in its grid of streets c1967.

Life in West Reading

It is often thought that institutions, and football clubs are institutions too, take on something of the character of their buildings and surrounding area. What did the changing image of Reading the town and, in particular, the district of West Reading hold for the Reading Football Club, late of Kings Meadow (1871-78), Reading Cricket ground Sonning (1878-82), Coley Park (1882-89) and Caversham (1889-96)?

To me the area around Elm Park was like a living "Observer Book of Small Town Life". It contained everything that was ordinary but all jumbled up in a way that you didn't know quite what was around the next corner. To the south of Elm Park, across the Tilehurst Road some of the housing is rather grand and detached. To the south-west lies the great, green sward of Prospect Park, a home of local football and much other sport besides. In all the other directions stood rows of red-brick terrace houses and the sheer concentration and proximity of them must surely have been the greatest influence on the surroundings of Elm Park.

As I grew up there in the 1960s the area still resembled a kind of Orwell's England, with its dark sweetshops, newsagents with out-of-date comics, grids of streets of near identical houses, jam factories, bottling plants, printworks, chip shops. As time passed people moved on. The streets became overparked, the roads clogged, the jobs fewer and more old-fashioned. The Oxford Road took on a tawdry lino and late night food feel, the encapsulation of 'the seedy averageness' for which the BBC and its original fly-on-the-wall documentary "The Wilkins Family" had made the town noted in the 1970s. Reading boomed to the East and the South while the West, like the football club, became trapped in the past.

By the 1980s, West Reading had become one of those areas that is among the last to rise in the economic cycle and among the first to fall. But Oxford Road, its main thoroughfare, remains full of entrepreneurs willing to have a go, though tattooists replace tailors and sex shops stand out more than sign-makers. Ironically, as the Reading Football Club left Elm Park, the West Reading regeneration programme began.

 The 20th century image of the town of Reading is coloured by two of the town's main 19th century economic materials: brick and biscuit, as flat, trivial and everyday as you can get.

Huntley & Palmer's Biscuit Factory, Reading.

Millions of biscuits, thousands of bricks.

The two materials metaphorically came together in the giant red-brick built Huntley & Palmers biscuit factory ('a town within a town' that once employed a quarter of the town's workforce) that dominated for 70 years the views from the train, the river and the canal. Houses the company built out of local brick for its workers in Newtown to the East, and similar houses in West Reading and by the Caversham Road, gave Reading a dark-red industrial hue. The immediate area surrounding Elm Park is of a part with this, patterned red brick houses with grey slate roofs stacked like rows of opened packets of biscuits up the slope of the Thames valley from the Oxford Road to the Tilehurst Road. A prospect swamped in brick and fuelled by biscuit; an unremarkable townscape of late Victorian and Edwardian terraced houses for respectable working folk.

In a sense Reading has the 'misfortune' to lie in one of the most prosperous regions of Europe, to be this banal brick town in comparison to the surrounding world famous delights of Henley, Windsor, Ascot and Oxford. Reading is uncharacteristic of its region. It is, along with towns like Luton, Portsmouth or Gillingham, another that makes up that odd concept, the Industrial South. Reading has had a notoriously unfair press dating from the era of the move to Elm Park. The poet John Betjeman, an expert in these matters and one not known for pulling his punches as the residents of Slough would attest, said it was "A much maligned town …No town in the South hides its attractions more successfully from the visitor". One of the main charges against it is characterlessness.

'Readingness' is particularly hard to define. Here's my take on it. It is an elastic, plastic sort of town, continually changing. Because it is so happily and well located in a prosperous and agreeable hinterland it is able to adapt to suit the times. Thus it does not get trapped into a single easy to define epoch, industry or image. A thousand years ago, when military power was important, it was a key position in the struggle against the Danes. In mediaeval times, when spirituality was the vital concern, Reading Abbey was one of the most prestigious centres. In the era of burgeoning trade that followed, Reading was a key player in the cloth industry. In the political cauldron of the 17th century Reading played host to Parliament and to key constitutional debates after the Civil War. When the Industrial Age came, Reading, without the natural resources of coal or iron, adapted and produced a world leading industry in biscuit-making. In the post-industrial age Reading has embraced the retail and financial revolutions and now its railway line and motorways are lined by the offices of the ground-breaking international companies of the global Information Age.

Reading works for those who come to it for work, for a new start, a new life, free from the tyrannies of no jobs, criminal gangs, exclusion by accent or domination by a narrow wealthy elite.

4th Division action from the air c1972.

It gave those that came in from say South Wales, Doncaster, Stoke and later from Dublin, Bridgetown and Karachi a chance to join with the spirit and the economy of the day. It works because companies come here to use the brains and will of its people. It is a place where the bright or resourceful without much to their name can get on in life.

Reading is something of a transit town where it is rare for a family to stay three generations. People here move in, move up and move out, just people having a go on their own in an unfriendly world. My parents' generation moved in. My generation moved out. You don't get any credit for getting on in the town of Reading and you don't tend to give it back either, not like Liverpool or Glasgow.

As one commentator said, "Reading is useful, very useful but it has no charm". Indeed, one of its most useful town centre thoroughfares is still unpretentiously known as Smelly Alley. It is a prosperous, workaday town, too busy ever to have needed one of those ad campaigns of the 'Glasgow's miles better' type to attract unnecessary tourists and traffic. These places, not just specifically Glasgow, aren't better. Reading is. That's why people come here. Reading people know that but they hear something else all the time, about how 'grotty', 'horrid' or 'dull' their beneficent town is. Inevitably this affects the way locals and newcomers see things.

Elm Park itself was partly built on an old brickworks and the soil was largely clay. It suits. It is an apt material. Clay is what the tiles of Tilehurst came from and what went in the kilns of Rose Kiln Lane. Clay, like the people here, feels indestructible, dogged, yet unaspirational, dull even. Like Sirrell's second-hand shop, Floorcraft and the 555 Fish Bar and many other shops down the Oxford Road, it sticks around.

Somehow this milieu, these surroundings, must impinge and affect the course of the club's history. Reading, as a town and a football club, has lacked self-confidence in its image all through the 20th century and been all too willing to look at people from elsewhere, who seem smarter or harder, for its leadership. There has never been enough professional football nearby for there to be a strong local football culture or an old mates' football 'mafia' like you get in Scotland, the North East or London. Reading football people are not as well-connected and therefore not as well respected. Reading Football Club has generally looked for outside guidance. We seem to have had relatively few local players compared with other clubs. In my time as a fan, 8 of its 11 managers have come from either Scotland or the North East or London. Only one, Maurice Evans, is what you could call local (and extremely popular) and speaks the way some of us do.

West Reading, close to encroaching onto the Elm Park turf.

So 'experts' from elsewhere came to mould us 'clay beings', to enliven our football lives with their big city brightness or coal-field connections. One after another they came down to our football 'outpost'. They arrived with probably a sigh at our cramped ground, crammed in its brick-dull grid. They sat in those cluttered, claustrophobic, windowless, wooden offices under the main stand, desperate to mould success out of us and a passport back to 'Big Football Country' for themselves before our clayiness smothered them. After the war it smothered them all except Ted Drake and Mark McGhee.

And, in the meantime, the passengers between Bristol or Oxford and London continued to look down from the railway embankments on to the narrow streets, plain houses and small factories, to think of them as a discountable drabness, a nothingness, not even pitiable, and probably to think of the football club set in its midst in, of course, the same rather contemptuous manner. Reading fans' frustration in being seen this way gave vent to our joy on the days and nights our team actually turned over some more 'media-friendly' outfits. The tragedy of losing the 1995 play-off final was that we could never confront the glittering world of the Premiership in these streets, never see fans of those top clubs walking down the Oxford Road in the vague hope of getting a ticket, and a soaking on the Town End, and never say to them 'awright, mate' knowing full well that, for them, it was not.

With hindsight the closing of Huntley & Palmers in 1976 symbolised the passing of one age. The football club were no longer 'the Biscuitmen' and the ground that had fitted so well with the era of the brick and the biscuit, the bicycle and the bus, was becoming a backwater. We locals didn't care because Elm Park fitted our long held perceptions of the town and the club. But, as 'Greater' Reading became bigger, and the business of Reading more lucrative and scientific, the outsider must have seen a football ground smaller, older and more trapped in space and time than befitted the emerging city and region around it.

Jesse's stand, the Chicken Run, and the old East Stand c1920.

The Building of Elm Park

In terms of the town of Reading, Elm Park was a big deal, a major place. For an institution that single-mindedly stayed in the same place for over a century, this is not surprising. To people outside Berkshire, Elm Park is still probably the best known place name within Reading, its existence the subject of a quiz question ten thousand times or more. If your definition of a tourist attraction is a place where non-locals pay to get in, then Elm Park has probably been Reading's biggest tourist attraction.

There were almost certainly men who fought in the Crimean War (1853-6) and watched football in Elm Park. There will probably be people living 250 years later, in 2100, who can recall watching Reading play there. The turnstiles, one of which pre-dated even Elm Park's foundation, have probably admitted upwards of 20 million match goers. 14 million have watched Football League matches and 1 million FA Cup ties. The Southern League games, the War League games, the League Cup, the Reserves, the 'A' team, the friendlies, the testimonials, the international matches, the Southern Floodlit Cup, the Simod Cup and all the rest of the minor and sponsored trophies, the ground share with Wokingham, the local leagues' cup finals and the schoolboy matches; they probably add up to another 5 million. And there were the military tournaments, the donkey derby, the horseback wrestling, the Freddie and the Dreamers concert, the Jehovah's Witnesses convention, American football, Rugby Union and all the other various activities that have taken place, including an exhibition bout featuring reigning World Heavyweight Champion Joe Louis.

People by the hundreds have had their births announced there over the tannoy, marriages have been consummated on the pitch(!), people have died in the ground and people's ashes have been scattered over it. One afternoon I was waiting in the Fred May lounge to see a club official when I was joined by three rather quiet, elderly ladies. "New midfield?" I quipped to my man when he showed up. He clenched his teeth, took them away, came back and told me they were an ash-scattering party. Aargh.

Elm Park was part of the heartbeat and the business of West Reading, it helped define the area and quickened the pace of life within it. For 30 years the floodlights announced its presence to all who travelled through Reading by rail. Today there are many that cannot drive down the Tilehurst Road, past its space, without averting their eyes or flinching and grieving a little.

Reading Vs Bournemouth again 1955. The South Bank roof awaits completion.

Though Elm Park existed in a late Victorian setting, the Elm Park most of us knew was not Victorian at all. Effectively there were two generations of Elm Park stands and terraces. The first generation saw Reading through the Southern League years, Division Three (South) and to promotion to Division Two in 1926. The structures were gradually replaced, taking over 30 years to become the Elm Park we knew from 1957 onwards. Virtually nothing of the original buildings survived to the 1990s.

The Elm Park of 1896-1926 had small wooden stands, rickety roofs, enamel advertising hoardings, shallow cinder bank terracing and railings rather than walls around the pitch. Built on poorly draining clay, Elm Park was 'very soft' in the centre and resisted improvements for some years. It was described, in 1902, as being "by no means favourable to a scientific display".

Councillor Jesse built the main stand, which seated about 700 on wooden benches and with a great many slender pillars obstructing the view. This stand occupied the central portion of the North side, set in somewhat from a corrugated iron fence that ran along Norfolk Road. Frank Orton, the current Club President and a descendant of Jesse's, remembers that "He wanted the main stand entrance to be on the Tilehurst Road with a double decker stand, but his fellow councillors would not allow it." This explains why, for over a century, the spectators who paid most got the sun in their eyes! A covered enclosure, nicknamed the 'Chicken Run', was built to the left of the grandstand, where later A and B stands were. This roofed enclosure carried on around to cover the northern half of the Town End. Opposite the main stand on the halfway line (that is, what became the centre of the South Bank) it appears there was a flight of ornamental stone stairs acting as a rather grand gangway.

On the Tilehurst End and the South Bank, spectators would have stood on shallow terracing, perhaps still turf perhaps cinder buttressed by wooden supports out in the open (though they all wore hats in those days). The principal access to the new ground by public transport was by tram down the Oxford Road and by foot up Kensington Road. Entrance was only possible from the Norfolk Road side and in winter kick-offs would have been at 2pm.

In 1919 Mr Spalding, a prospective Parliamentary candidate, donated £700 for the building of a roof over the rear portion of the South Bank and, the following year, with League football arriving, the pitch was levelled and new managerial offices built under the stand. Reading played their first Football League home match on 1st September 1920 at Elm Park and never played a home League match anywhere else until 22nd August 1998. In the early 1920s, Elm Park offered supporters fairly restricted views and little shelter against the rain.

A packed post-war crowd...

...passively watches a Reading corner.

The Tilehurst End under construction 1957.

No more than one in three fans would have had a roof over their heads and there were less than a thousand seats. Attendances would vary wildly in those early days, the highest being a gate of 24,354 to watch a promotion battle against Bristol City in March 1926.

With promotion to Division Two secured in May 1926 and Reading now at last Full Members of the Football League (rather than non-voting Associates) and more in the public eye, it was time to bring Elm Park up to standard. The Chelsea programme had recently commented, "a first impression of Elm Park is rather disconcerting. The numerous stands and shelters take ones mind back to some of the suburbs of Ypres (a town destroyed in the First World War)". The main stand was way out-of-date and the roof over the Town End seats had recently blown away in a gale, so a new grandstand was built on the site of the old, opening on 13th November 1926 and lasting until Elm Park's final game. It then held around 4,000, mostly seated on unnumbered benches. The following season, 1926/27, was the most successful yet, with the club finishing 14th in Division Two, reaching the FA Cup Semi-Final and gates rising to an average of 13,389, the 8th highest for the Division. Elm Park's record attendance of 33,042 squeezed in for the Fifth Round cup-tie against Brentford. Reading stayed up for 5 seasons, still our longest spell yet at this level, and won the affection of the town. Many supporters including famously John Arlott came by bicycle, and residents in Norfolk Road used to charge a penny a bike for using their front garden as bikesheds. Others marched behind the brass band all the way from the Wokingham Road to the ground.

Arlott was the best cricket commentator there ever was and the most famous Reading supporter of his day. "You have an interesting but vulgar voice" his BBC employer once said, and how that fits with a Reading fan. Writing in 1950 he recalled a cup-tie against Aston Villa in 1929, "There were ordinary chairs on the grass inside the barriers, so that the purchasers of special tickets could sit near the touchline. So heavy was the rain that the legs of the chairs sank into the mud; small boys were passed over the heads of the chairsitters lest they should be crushed."

In 1930, Reading Football Supporters' Club was founded and over the next thirty years it played an important part in fundraising and labouring to improve facilities for the ordinary terrace fan. The loyalty and effort of supporters was amazing. Through tea dances, whist drives and many other activities they raised, in the equivalent of today's money, about a million pounds. The Town End terrace was improved in 1931 following a 'one shilling' scheme, the centre portion of the South Bank was roofed in 1936 at a cost of over £1,000 and the tannoy system was installed in 1946. A 'twenty thousand shilling fund' was launched in 1946 to complete the roofing of the South Bank. This was done in two further stages, 1949 and 1956.

Scotland training at the old Tilehurst End.

Pre First World War Elm Park.

Record League crowd, 1949.

For the most part the directors were more concerned to finance the playing side in order to get back to Division Two. In 10 out of the 13 seasons following relegation in 1931, Reading finished in the top six but were never first at a time when only the top club went up. Under the dynamic chairmanship of William Lee, the club itself had major development plans in the late 1940s. As football boomed in the post-war period and Reading's average gates rose to their highest ever level of 15,000, he commissioned, in 1949, a leading firm of architects to redesign Elm Park. New turnstiles and accessways were built on the South Bank side and the remainder of the old roof, dating from 1919, was demolished. There were new dressing rooms, office space and baths, but the grander plans, firstly re-covering the Town End and secondly building a double-decker stand over the South Bank, never came to fruition. The tight post-war regulations on the availability of new building materials and the lack of enough friends in high places may have been the causes. However, Reading were among the earlier floodlight pioneers. The inaugural match under lights took place on 6th October 1954 against Racing Club de Paris in front of 13,000 fans and the BBC cameras which televised the second-half live.

Reading's failure to win promotion in 1952 after so many near misses spelt the end first for manager Ted Drake, who left to take Chelsea to their only Championship, then chairman Lee and finally the best of the players. The mid 1950s were a flat period for the club on the pitch but the Supporters' Club continued their good work, assisted occasionally by the players, by rebuilding the Tilehurst End. Work began in April 1957 replacing the rotting, weed-infested railway sleepers with four-inch-high concrete steps.

In 1958 the old Divisions Three North and South were superseded by the new national Divisions Three and Four. Reading gained a place in Division Three from which there were now be two promotion places available. Elm Park was probably in its peak ever condition at this point. The Tilehurst End was brand new, the South Bank recently renovated and covered, and nothing anywhere much in the place more than 30 years old. By the standards of the day it was tidy, compact, yet of a decent capacity, generally given as 30,000. Some grounds in the division still had cinder terracing and no floodlights while Elm Park was ready for Second Division status. So how did it come to be condemned to decay and derision, death and demolition?

A goal in the early 1980s dog days.

The Decay of Elm Park

For the quarter of a century after 1958 Reading Football Club grew weaker and weaker until it almost died in 1983. Promotion back to Division Two, which supporters had ceased to regard as the club's rightful place, was never a strong possibility in this period. By the early 1960s the club had settled down to life in the middle of Division Three. A complacent gerontocracy on the board held sway and there were no more serious attempts to improve Elm Park. Virtually nothing major or obviously noticeable to the naked eye changed. The general decline in crowd figures did not justify any significant investment.

Modest improvements were made: more refreshment points, the first souvenir shop and the installing of tip-up seats throughout the stand, which meant the end of the old practice of hiring individual cushions to save your backside from the rigours of the bench seating. (These were also useful as missiles for the disgruntled.) In 1965 the Supporters Club opened a bar underneath the stand, which was later taken over as the sponsors lounge, and a year later Hospital Radio Reading set up a studio deep in the bowels of the Tilehurst End.

With the coming of a new manager, Jack Mansell, in 1969, things began to look up again. The original floodlights, despite homespun additions of lamps mounted on trolley bus poles, were now substandard and replaced in the close season with 'proper' floodlight pylons as seen at major clubs. With crowds briefly back to 15,000 there was again talk of a double-decker stand on the Tilehurst Road side and a pub on the corner of the ground to match the kind of developments going up at places like QPR and Swindon. But a surprise relegation and five years in the Fourth Division put paid to the need for all that. Elm Park, which in the football programmes of the 1960s was customarily described as 'a well-appointed ground', was now beginning to look a bit past it.

Another phenomenon of that era had a permanent impact on the look of Elm Park. There had been isolated instances of crowd trouble in the 1960s but by 1970 the problem of hooliganism was almost constant. The first action the club took was to erect fences down the terracing at either end of the South Bank thus separating the ground into four separate parts. Previously fans had been able to walk around the ground from behind one goal to the other but this freedom was no more. Strangely, it was another 10 years before the Town End was officially designated for away supporters. In the meantime there were plenty of hairy afternoons with rival sets of fans encamped on either side of the South Bank.

Promotion 1976. "Oi Charlie, have a swig!".

Looking back with the benefit of hindsight it seems the authorities were amazingly casual about what went on in a football ground in those days. Tea was served in china mugs and the Supporters' Club were forever moaning in the programme about fans leaving them on the terraces to be smashed. I can remember, as a kid, collecting loads of empties from the Tilehurst End and taking them back to the Corona bottling plant to get the refunds. Later I was once let out of the stand to go to the Spread Eagle for a half-time pint! It would appear you could bring whatever you wanted to into the ground. A friend did his party shopping on the way to one really boring game. Sat on the terrace steps at half-time with several bottles of wine around him, he commented, "what this game needs is a corkscrew". As for the missiles the skinheads brought in....

Twice, in 1976 and 1979, Reading were promoted from Division Four but on neither occasion was there finance or ambition in the boardroom for this to be a springboard for a challenge on Division Two. Then, in the early 1980s, all the energy seemed to drain completely out of the club. Talented players were sold and not replaced. Elm Park itself was increasingly neglected, forlorn and empty. Gates fell to an all-time low of 1,713 in October 1982. It was about this time that Simon Inglis, the writer who made his name writing about football grounds, made a visit and subsequently pronounced Elm Park the most boring ground in the League. And if you saw it empty then, with all the 'dull Reading' imagery in your head, maybe that's the way it looked. In later editions of his book he toned down his negative viewpoint.

There was a reason for this decay. The directors had lost any enthusiasm for the club. Behind the scenes ageing chairman Frank Waller was negotiating with press baron and Oxford United owner Robert Maxwell to merge their two clubs and, in theory at least, to build a new joint stadium in Didcot. Whilst the Didcot stadium was always unlikely it was probable that Elm Park would have been bulldozed and sold off for re-development and that would have meant the end of first class football in Reading, sometime in 1983. And if it had been the end, if Elm Park had died aged 87 rather than 102, posterity's verdict on the place would have been far different. For Elm Park still had 15 years of truly vital life left. In its old age, Elm Park was to become much more loved and appreciated, a place that became a fascinating counterpoint to the football age in which it existed. In 1983 maybe only a few thousand cared; by 1998 the number was much, much greater.

Promotion 1979. The longest unbeaten defence in League history (1103 minutes) get tight.

Elm Park's Lively Old Age

In 1983 few would have dared predict the tumultous success of Reading in the 15 years after the club nearly disappeared. When Roger Smee rescued the club from Robert Maxwell's clutches and became chairman in May 1983 his ambition was to move to a new ground. The Reading Chronicle reported at the time his desire for a "10,000 all-seater stadium in the Smallmead area which would be linked to commercial use and incorporate a leisure complex". At the time this was a very progressive stance to take especially as Elm Park was far from the worst ground around. No League club had moved home for nearly 30 years and the first of the new generation all-seaters (Scunthorpe) was not opened until 1988. By 1984, the notion that Reading Football Club would move to Smallmead was written in local government's Kennet Valley Plan. Elm Park, as a football stadium, was now publicly on the endangered list and no longer a candidate for ground redevelopment.

Yet, despite still looking much the same, a lot of work had to go into Elm Park in its last years. The new, spring-cleaning Smee regime brought a wholesale repainting of the ground, with bright blue-and-white replacing the dingy grey breeze block and cast iron. In the 1983/84 season Reading were again promoted from the Fourth Division then made a respectable showing in Division Three. But attendances were desperately low, averaging only 3,700. For 6 years between 1979 and 1985 there was no League gate higher than 10,000 at Elm Park. In the country at large football was reaching the depths of its unpopularity. The televised hooligan excesses were followed in quick order by the Heysel and Bradford fire disasters of 1985. The subsequent Popplewell Report into the Bradford tragedy had significant implications for Elm Park and, in particular, its 1926-built wooden stand.

For the start of the 1985/86 season, smoking was banned in the seated areas, the gangways were widened and the top seven rows were cordoned off as being too far from the exits in case of fire. These seats at the back of the stand were replaced the following year by 12 executive boxes. Over a thousand seats were lost and the total capacity of Elm Park was initially reduced to just 8,000.

As the first match attracted less than 4,000 this did not seem to be a problem. But Reading kept on winning every game and soon faced the bizarre situation of having to lock fans out of a match against Bolton with only 8,000 in the ground. By late October frantic efforts were made to increase capacity and 'well over' 13,000 saw the game that ended Reading's record-breaking 13 games winning streak.

Opening day 1985-86, but it's the end for Row N.

In May 1986, Reading were promoted back to the old Second Division they had left as long ago as 1931. More minor improvements followed. A clumsy-looking fire escape was erected in Norfolk Road for the benefit of the executive boxes. The Family Enclosure was moved to E Stand, the Tilehurst Road turnstiles were demolished and re-sited nearer the South Bank and the long awaited Royals Rendezvous, a large bar for supporters, was built behind the South Bank on the Tilehurst Road.

At the same time, and about 15 years too late, the authorities began to make serious, yet misguided, attempts to address the hooligan problem. Elm Park had witnessed some terrible scenes in the early 1980s. One so-called solution was for fans to show identity cards on entry. Reading embraced this scheme all too enthusiastically as a pioneer and fans had to show cards to get on to the South Bank. Our ground-breaking participation was commemorated by a circular, engraved memorial plaque set in the floor of the passage that ran along the back of the South Bank, where it was frequently covered by the puddles that gathered there. A vast amount of money was ultimately wasted on this computerised scheme and on more and higher fences to keep both home and away supporters from the pitch.

After two seasons in Division Two, Reading were relegated and almost went down again the following season. Crowds were down to 4,000 again and once more the money and desire from the board seemed to have evaporated. Smallmead was just a grey cloud drifting on the horizon rather than a week-to-week part of fans' thinking. And then in April 1989 there was yet another disaster when 96 fans were crushed to death at Hillsborough.

Four days after Hillsborough I went to a meaningless Reading -Wigan match for no other reason than to take part in the minute's silence with my fellow football fans. It hung very heavy that night as we thought of death on the terraces. But Hillsborough was also the death *of* the terraces and with it the death of Elm Park. The subsequent Taylor Report ended both the authorities' insistence on high fencing and identity cards. However, it also recommended all-seater stadia in the top two divisions by 1994 and even for the lower divisions by 1999.

The sums were done on the number of seats a converted Elm Park could take and it was about 9,000 and it should have had roofs at either end. Even with this rebuilding there would still be the parking constraints, the difficulty of providing quality accommodation for the increasingly important sponsors and modern offices for ever-growing backroom staff. There was no will in the boardroom to save and redevelop Elm Park now.

Horrix and Hicks (Reading's scorers on the day were Senior and Sanchez !).

The Smallmead site, theoretically on offer down by the motorway, was much more financially attractive and architecturally adaptable in the long term.

In the short term Reading were down in the Third Division and on their uppers again. Smee's property company and therefore chairmanship was one of the early victims of the '90s recession (he resigned in late 1990) and the club were again near to closure before John Madejski, the publisher of AutoTrader, stepped in to save it. When Madejski became Chairman he saw a new ground as the one thing that could cause a transformation and take the club out of the lower divisions on a near-permanent basis. Without it, the future would be one of small-time struggle. Reading had to catch the all-seater bus and the only destination that was ever mentioned was Smallmead.

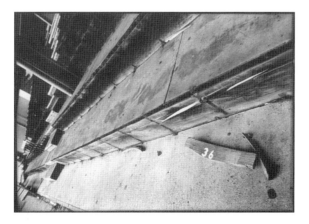

On Our Way to Smallmead

Quite when the notion Reading might move to Smallmead started is difficult to trace. One source has Reading's speedway promoter, Reg Fearman, as the promulgator of a 'sports mecca' in the Smallmead area as far back as the early 1970s. It is worth following the track of Reading Racers speedway team over the past couple of decades because its course often runs astonishingly parallel to that of Reading Football Club.

Built for greyhound racing in 1931, Reading Stadium was situated on the crossroads of Oxford Road, Norcot Road and Scours Lane on what at that time was probably the edge of town, less than a mile west of Elm Park. The first meeting attracted a crowd of about 4,000 and, as an institution for the working and betting man, it stuck around quietly like so much of West Reading, for years. One half knew it was there but we grew up in a dull, brown, closed off world, full of things you couldn't do and places you could not even see into. Anything remotely tempting – pubs, bookies, barbers, Elm Park – had to be discreet and uninviting. Local back streets were dotted with 'shops' behind frosted, opaque windows bearing the deterring words 'trade sales only'. Reading Stadium managed both to obey and flaunt these rules. For years I went past it, not knowing quite what went on behind its grand double gates. But you could sense from the brashness of its lettering and the style of its entrance that it would not be something parents approved of. It spoke of America, that disapproved-of America, of hot-dogs, ice cream soda, war comics, motorbikes, even drive-ins – the ultimate consumer sin.

Reading Racers opened as a speedway team at the Reading Stadium in 1968. In a town starved of sporting success, with a

stale and listless football club, it offered a new outlet. Within a couple of years the Racers were promoted and crowds of 10,000 were not uncommon. In 1973 the Racers brought the national championship of a team sport to Reading for the first time but they also knew that the lease on the stadium had run out. Despite having the most impressive sports stand in the town it was knocked down in months and the Racers had to hibernate for a year and a half.

Away from all human society and on the cheap, Reading Racers re-emerged in April 1975 in a place few Reading folk had ever heard of – Smallmead! At the turn of the century the area had become the home of the town's sewage works but looking at a late 1950s map there is no mention of the name itself. It were just all fields and drainage ditches and Wind Pump (disused) down there. By the mid 1970s a Small Mead Road has emerged as a continuation of Island Road pointing in the direction of the sublimely unromantically named Farm No.2 (only in Reading – or East Germany!).

On a 1995 map there are two unconnected halves of a Smallmead Road, the newer part running past Smallmead Farm (formerly Farm No.2). In the 1970s, and indeed far beyond, there was not much call to go to Smallmead apart from disposing of all manner of waste, be it household, human, automotive or building. The area was locked, with no through roads, between the Kennet&Avon Canal to the north, the M4 to the south, the Basingstoke railway line to the west and the Basingstoke Road industrial estate to the east. It was bisected by the Foudry Brook, a substantial stream, and generally suffused with the odours of the nearby sewage works. It was the urban equivalent of the cupboard under the stairs, the place where the council put things they did not want anybody else to see (or smell). No one lived within half-a-mile radius. For non-speedway lovers it was as ideal a spot in a town as you could find for a speedway stadium!

And there, all faded blue and weather-beaten, looking like the oldest 24 year-old in Reading (some feat in itself!), it still stands today, but now with the grandness of the Madejski Stadium on its southern horizon for company. I went to Smallmead's opening speedway night, thinking some terrible banishment had been exacted on the Racers that placed them beyond Rose Kiln Lane, then a dead-end full of car breakers yards; behind Gillette's, the faraway factory on the edge of town. They were still building the stadium as we approached! It had been a record wet winter, the builders said. The stadium was a quite different, rather cold experience and I never went back to see the Racers again.

Whenever the prospect of Reading Football Club leaving Elm Park was raised, the destination was always Smallmead and not specifically a separate stadium from the speedway, even in the early 1990s. One time club chairman Frank Waller was the first to suggest ground-sharing in 1982. The lack of enthusiasm amongst supporters for this 'banishment' was clear. What was not clear, and why should it have been, was the effect of the totality of the plans to open up and develop the whole area through building a major new road. This would change the game completely.

19th century turnstiles.

The Final Years

By 1992 a number of pressures were combining to force Reading to make the decision to vacate Elm Park. From a legislative point of view, the club had only a maximum of 7 years before having to go all-seater. The Football Licensing Authority already had concerns about the safety of the Town End terrace. Around the country the major clubs were already undertaking massive stadium improvement programmes and some of the lesser lights were already giving up their old grounds for newly built all-seaters elsewhere. As a football club, Reading could not continue to stand still while the reconstruction revolution happened around them. Meanwhile, Reading Borough Council's plans for the A33 Relief Road, which would open up the whole Smallmead area to easy motorway access, were set to get underway. In September of that year, among several others, I was invited by the council, in a professional capacity, to join in preliminary discussions about the development of sports stadia in the town. The big decisions had already been taken. It was now a question of when, who with and how much.

In December 1993, with Reading back on top of Division Two (as it had become), an unsurprising public announcement was made of a definite decision to move to a completely new, purpose built stadium at Smallmead as soon as possible. Shortly after, almost as if to emphasise the point, the gates of Elm Park were shut with only 11,000 inside for the match against Stockport. Too many fans had arrived too unexpectedly for the security operation to cope. There were continuing signs of recovery in the game at large, not just at Reading. Some of the new fans were not the kind easily accommodated at Elm Park. It was, at times, easier to get your boy into Eton than get him a ticket as a Junior Royal! Managing Director Mike Lewis came to one Supporters Club meeting and tried to encourage some enthusiasm for the new stadium by saying that car parking would be much easier. The dyed-in-the-wool fans did not have much to say one way or the other. No joy, no protest, just a resigned acceptance of the necessary loss.

In 1994 Reading stylishly made it back into what is now called the First Division. Under the conditions of the Taylor Report Reading, as a First Division club, had three years grace (1994-97) in which to go all-seater. As there was no intention of ever improving Elm Park, apart from some safety work to raise the capacity of the Town End terrace, all funds and grants were saved for the new ground. To general astonishment the following season we came within a few minutes of making it all the way to the top division for the first time ever.

Elm Park could have finally had its moment in the limelight as the last, old-fashioned terraced ground in the top division.

Best seats in the house.

While the national press were beginning to notice and criticise what they saw as Elm Park's 'ramshackle', 'rusting', antiquity, for fans from many clubs it would have been a welcome counterpoint to the increasingly standardised all-seater stadia of the big clubs.

For others it would have caused problems. In the run-in to the end of the season Reading played in front of crowds of 12,000 plus. Before the Bolton match one young female fan wrote to the Evening Post about being frightened by crush outside the Tilehurst Road turnstiles. In the play-off semi-final, the Town End was temporarily split down the middle to house more Reading fans and all the Tranmere support was asked to use just the ladies' loos. John Madejski floated the idea in the press that, if promoted, Reading might play some of their top home games at grounds in London. Sadly, the Premiership was never to come to Elm Park but we had a sense of what the football world might have thought when Reading drew Manchester United at home in the FA Cup 4th Round in January 1996.

The tie was played on a bitterly cold afternoon, the biggest of only four ties to take place that day. Fleet Street sent their finest, now comfortably accustomed to the post-Taylor Premiership stadia, to report back. Even Match of the Day cameras turned up, the first and last time a match at Elm Park was fully covered by them. If the football world was to give Elm Park a valediction, a funeral oration on the sports pages, then this was it.

The Guardian called Elm Park "a pre-Taylor museum, fifty years past its sell-by date". The Times saw "a classic four-cornered shack, roofed with corrugated metal that rises from a sea of little red houses from which the front room is separated from the street by a single door. Football Country. Elm Park, Reading is a throwback". The Times may have walked down Brunswick Street but I can think of no other road that fits the description precisely.

The Daily Telegraph wrote, "Wooden stands, a sandy pitch, a park bench for the Manchester United management and a tangerine sun setting behind corrugated roofs, dusted with snow... Call it naivety, or even snobbishness but it came as a jolt to discover such an old-fashioned and unprepossessing ground just a promotion struggle away from the Premiership... it could pass for somebody's house. The thud of old floorboards under your feet and impossible queues for toilets were an invitation to drift back to your football childhood". Except it was our fortnightly reality.

As a sentimentalist and a romantic you need to see the evidence with your own eyes to be finally convinced.

"Champions !" - The South Bank in full cry, 1994.

One afternoon, only months from the end, long-standing groundsman Fred Neate (in the employ of the Football Club since 1956) took me round Elm Park and showed me what was happening beneath it. Underneath the terraces the clay was still moving, trying to burst and shake itself free of football. We stood over the corner flag looking down the Town End terrace to Norfolk Road. All the terrace steps should be in straight lines but they weren't, they were about as straight as the waves coming up the beach, some only a few inches wide in places. In the stand some of the tip-up seats didn't tip up because the stand was actually leaning slightly towards the pitch. All the bowing walls, the asbestos roofing of the South Bank, all the continuous maintenance of the crush barriers spending thousands every other season to allow people to stand in the wet for £9 – all this was the necessary civil engineering reality. Time had caught Elm Park up and time was eating money that could be put to better use.

Terrace Life.

THE FORTRESS YEARS

1925/26	16	5	0	49-16
1931/32	19	1	1	65-21
1933/34	17	4	0	60-13
1934/35	16	5	0	52-20
1935/36	18	0	3	52-20
1937/38	17	2	2	44-21
1951/52	19	2	2	72-23
1975/76	19	3	1	42-09
1978/79	19	3	1	49-08
1983/84	17	6	0	51-14

Awright ?

What Made Elm Park Special ?

What makes any place special is not just the building itself but the memories you yourself bring to it. That's why Elm Park will always be special to Reading fans but probably not many others. Each supporter's story will be slightly different. The programme for the final League match and 'Elm Park Echoes' – a splendid collection of pieces assembled by ex-fanzine editor Tony Ella and on sale the same day – covered many of those different personal perspectives.

During the last season at Elm Park, in order to make those who cared a little more conscious of what we were about to lose, I slipped a series of descriptive snippets into the club programme. They recalled some of the quirky, idiosyncratic parts of the experience of going to the match at the old ground, just shards of memory, glimpses from unusual angles. Slightly adapted, here are some memories that may strike a chord or two.

From the Spread Eagle corner, Elm Park loomed like a grimy fortress: bleak, concrete walls topped with broken glass (long since illegal but so?), battered metal doors fronted by uniformed men, overhead an intricate melange of wires, cables and pipes, look-outs silhouetted in the floodlit glare. And no sign of an elm tree anywhere.

There was the curious phenomenon of the unseen slope down Norfolk Road. To reach pitch level on entering Elm Park, away fans at the Town End had to climb a flight of steps yet, at the Tilehurst End, home fans walked straight in at ground level.

Architecturally the most basic of grounds, Elm Park made one tiny concession to unique decorative features, the serrated wooden pelmet that ran the length of the grandstand roof since 1926 and last bore the 'Free Ads' advert.

The thunder of feet stamped in encouragement on the wooden floors of the stand as Reading pressed forward late on in an important match. "G'arn, you Rs" growled the hunched and jacketed rows while below the tea ladies, packing up for the afternoon, flinched at the noise just a few feet above them.

The second-half sun slanted down from over English Martyrs church straight into the faces of the main stand. As Reading attacked the Tilehurst End, in unison E Stand, D Stand, and C Stand raised arms and programmes to shield their eyes.

Cables, struts, blokes and blocks.

There was a familiar three part sound that will be missed in the new stadium. Firstly a hush as the crowd momentarily caught its breath, then an unceremonious 'boink' as the clearance dropped on the roof and finally a muffled hurrah from the terraces as it disappeared into the road behind.

In Elm Park, unlike modern, enclosed wraparound stadia, the fan was very conscious of the town the team was playing for. Maroon Corporation buses passed within sight of the pitch, a pub and a church peeped over the walls, familiar Reading red-brick encircled the ground and away on the north-east horizon protruded the sodium lights and the big office blocks of the town centre.

The Town End used to be the better maintained and more popular of the two ends but, given to away fans, it came to feel cut-off and neglected. The weather came down the valley into your face more often than not and the pitch seemed to slope a little into your feet. But the view from the back was good and a luxuriant creeper had burst under the plastic roof of the toilets.

Holding about 7,000, the South Bank had probably become, by process of the elimination of the others, the largest and most versatile terrace in the League. It offered views high and low, close to one goal or the other, under cover or outside, and packed in with the lads or on your own behind a pillar.

Round the back of the South Bank, where it once joined the Town End, there was a kind of Berlin Wall, a concourse ending in chained, rusty iron gates and concrete weed-strewn oblivion where in more peaceful days fans walked at half-time from behind one goal to the other.'

There was a channel that ran along the back of the South Bank probably only 3 or 4 feet wide. At half-time it was full of familiar faces and jostling bodies "Awright?" "Awright" struggling in opposite directions as the crowd changed places, sought 'relief' or sustenance. It was always dark, cramped and usually puddled, even on the sunniest days.

On the wall right behind the Tilehurst goal you were so close to the pitch it was like watching and listening to players in a park. You were a couple of yards from taking part in a League match but the nearest you usually got to the action was avoiding miss-hit shots during the pre-match kick-in.

The sun slants down over English Martyrs Church.

The homeward crowd, clad in blue-and-white hoops, spilled quickly out of the brick walls like colourful sweets from a suddenly burst bag. A column of bobbing heads marched up Wantage Road between the rows of pollarded trees back to Tilehurst or cars to take them further.

Elm Park was an utterly unpretentious, shabby, uncompromising place. There was a physical tightness about it. Everything was compact, intense and close. It was built in the factory age and from Norfolk Road it looked like a factory, a place of some mysterious manufacture that did not give up its secrets lightly, that kept the world away behind frosted glass and shuttered gates. On the other side, from pitch level the South Bank seemed to lean over like the broadside of a war-weary battleship and from within came its barrages of cheers and volleys of sarcasm.

Of course, the mood and the atmosphere depended on the weather, the crowd and the score. Within the space of a few games it could be one thing and then some other quite different experience. Elm Park on an empty Spring night with just 2,000 desperate souls forcing themselves to watch the fag-end of another failed season. Elm Park on a lazy sunny afternoon with 4,000 spread easily around - pleasantly half-asleep. Elm Park on a soft autumn evening with 8,000 stood about – lively and content. Elm Park in the gloom of a dank and muddy cup-tie afternoon with 10,000 - tensely poised. Elm Park on a winter's night with the rain drilling down on the rusty tin roofs with 18,000 – noisily blocked and pressed in together.

And besides the sights there were the sounds, the buzz of the crowd, the growl of anticipation when Gilkes got the ball in space, the angry silence that greeted an opposition goal, the moans and the brickbats of the disillusioned and, most of all, the songs of the South Bank. In truth, the best of the noise generated by the South Bank bounced back off the low roof into our own ears rather than out to the rest of the ground but on the occasions the whole side sung, it was a truly great racket.

And then the tastes. When my wife started coming to Elm Park, she asked a group of us whether we wanted anything to eat or drink at half-time and we looked at her as if she was mad. It had been so long ago that we decided that the quality of the food was inversely proportionate to the length of the queue and that anything more than one in front wasn't worth the bother. We'd forgotten it was even an option! And back in the days of penny-pinching economising of the 1980s, there were brands of food and drink supplied that you never saw anywhere else, like blue-coloured (or flavoured) Naris Fizz.

Fuelling the spirits.

Back street theatre.

"Rea – ding, Rea – ding, Rea – ding".

As for feelings, well, you never felt that cold on the South Bank but the rest of the ground could get as brass monkeys as anywhere in the land. And oddly I never recall feeling particularly crushed in Elm Park compared with some much bigger grounds I've stood in. I saw 3 games with over 22,000 in without any memorable discomfort. The worst time was in a crowd of nearly 19,000 against Luton in 1970, a match played in a continuous heavy downpour. I tried to get under the South Bank roof but, aged 14, I simply could not force my way into the rock-solid block of bodies and the pandemonium of noise, steam and smoke, Luton fans as well as Reading fans, and so turned back.

There were smells too, 3 basic smells: frying, piss and cigarettes. You could be unlucky and get a smelly fan too! Lord Justice Taylor made famous 'the stench of fried onions' when writing his report on the condition of football grounds in 1989 and Elm Park was proud to maintain that tradition to the end. Just so I, and hopefully she, can proudly say she once went to Elm Park, we took our four year old daughter to watch a reserve match. The first thing she noticed was the smokiness of the Rendezvous and the stands – "Poo, smoky" and the second, passing the C Stand toilets, was the overcoming stench of ...she squirmed and frowned trying to define this powerful, unknown experience before pronouncing – "Uuugh, ...Bacon?!" We let it go at that, but it was interesting to note what most caught a small child's attention.

Another lad, Sam aged 10, wrote to me about his impressions of the first League match he ever saw, the 4-2 win over Wolves in 1994, stood on a beer crate in the South Bank. "I was excited entering the stadium. I thought there would be seats there. It was a small stadium, I thought it would be bigger because I see bigger stadiums on the TV. It was very noisy. There was no fighting going on." Already the next generation's expectations were completely shaped by the TV experience of Premiership football – against which Elm Park was something quite different.

Rationally speaking, there was a lot wrong with Elm Park, but some people, many people, liked it that way. Rationally, almost all could afford a better, cleaner, more convenient 'product' and anyone wanting an afternoon's casual entertainment would certainly demand such. But, for a lot of football fans, rationality doesn't really come into it. Otherwise we would all be watching Man U on pay-per-view. There were two forces behind the growing sentimentality that attached itself to Elm Park in its final years.

Firstly, there was the 'old warrior' mentality of the long-suffering football fan who likes to take pains with his pleasure and, indeed, glory in them.

The long queues for tickets, the long walk to the ground, standing in the cold or wet, crushed and hungry, still all Jarrow Marchers at heart, it's all been part of the experience man and boy. John Arlott wrote of his support in the 20s, "the ground was about 18 miles from my home, it was a cycle ride, a hard one but worth it... if I could raise ten pence, six pence admission, two pence for a programme, a penny mineral on the way up and another on the return journey, I would be there". Those of us above the age of 20, we've all been there and learnt the terracecraft of where to queue, where to stand, who to avoid, of rushing to the bogs the moment the trainer comes on for a head injury, and all those now redundant 'skills'. All the problems you learnt to solve for yourself will now be solved for you and for the next easy come easy go generation.

Secondly, the 1990s saw the growth of the cult of 'laddism', exemplified by the TV comedy series 'Men Behaving Badly'. The elemental truth it played on was that blokes don't want to feel designed, sanitised, safe and polite all the time. As the worlds of work and commerce relentlessly take on those less masculine values, the rude and smelly darkness of a crumbling concrete bank under sheets of rusting tin became a fortnightly escape back to a simpler, grubbier past. Football's places had always been determinedly industrial and masculine, cavernous sheds made of harsh materials. But now there was something quite different on the horizon.

For a few months you could stand at a spot in the centre of Prospect Park, just short of the Mansion House, and see not only the doomed lights and grey roofs of Elm Park to the east but also the rising walls and girders of the Madejski Stadium to the south.

PART TWO   THE LAST SEASON

Asaba and Bullivant ready for the cameras.

Bullivant's Mission Possible

Reading started their 91st and final season at Elm Park as the bookies' favourites for relegation back to Division Two. Such a judgement flew in the face of the club's and its fans' new aspirations. The success of the previous 5 years and the knowledge that a new stadium was on the way had created an ambitious and hopeful football climate.

From the brink of closure in December 1990 John Madejski and, later, Mark McGhee had guided Reading to a surprising (16-1 at the bookies) Division Two Championship in 1994 and, without McGhee in the dug-out, almost crept into the Premiership in 1995. A window of opportunity presented itself to an unfancied side with few obvious stars finishing the season strongly. Reading were almost through that window and out into the golden pastures of the top division when a late Bolton goal yanked them back. Jimmy Quinn and Mick Gooding, as joint player-managers, had done a good job keeping McGhee's team going in the short-term but they did not have his touch in the transfer market or on the training ground. Under their management the next two seasons were relegation struggles, both won it must be said, but supporters sensed they did not have the ability to take the club forward in the way McGhee had done. In effect, they were neither good nor bad. They saw out their contracts and, with little support from the dressing room or the terraces, were asked to be on their way. Both were respected and liked as players but as managers they were sergeants and Reading now needed a general.

Finding such a general proved remarkably hard. There were 70 applicants and all sorts of names linked with the job from resolute ex-Southampton boss Dave Merrington to temperamental ex-German international Bernd Schuster. It seemed for a while that ex-Celtic manager Tommy Burns would join, but instead he took a coaching position at Newcastle. 7 close season weeks elapsed and the new season was fast approaching when an announcement was finally made. It was to be the Barnet manager Terry Bullivant. The Evening Post back page could say nothing more than 'It's Bullivant!' The Reading public, hyped and tantalised by exotic possibilities, was distinctly underwhelmed. "Terry Vol-au vent?" one passer-by famously said to a TV camera. Bullivant hardly helped his cause in his first interview by suggesting that if the position did not work out he would be happy to go back to being a London taxi-driver. Not the bold statement of ambition the people wanted to hear.

Bullivant had relatively little time for pre-season training and found forward Lee Nogan about to leave for Grimsby. The other two senior forwards, Stuart Lovell and Trevor Morley were both sidelined with career-threatening injuries as was club captain Barry Hunter. Then record signing Darren Caskey broke his leg in training. You could see the bookies' point.

Action from upon high...

...and from down below.

Reading Vs QPR beneath a bloody sky.

On the other hand, all Reading really wanted from the season was to avoid relegation so we could take First Division status to the new stadium. Unlike several rival sides, Reading had some financial resource, resource that allowed striker Carl Asaba to be bought from Brentford for £800,000 on the eve of the big kick-off. Bullivant's Mission Possible was simply to finish above any three of Bury, Crewe, Oxford, Stockport, Swindon, Port Vale, Tranmere, Huddersfield or Portsmouth, the likely drop candidates, or any other side that went duff during the season. 52 points would probably do it; 14 wins, 10 draws, 22 defeats, it didn't sound too awesome.

Elm Park was spruced up and ready to go. Its capacity was now 15,000 but there were only about 2,400 seats and corporate entertainment facilities were more village hall than city hotel.

The season began with a creditable, if fortunate, draw at newly promoted Bury, but five straight defeats followed, with only one goal scored. The home programme opened on a hot afternoon to a dull 0-1 defeat at the hands of oldest rivals Swindon. By the fourth game the on-loan players were coming in, always a worrying sign. Mark Robins, once of Manchester United, missed a chance in the opening minute at home against Bradford City and they went on to win 3-0. The media and then the crowd were already getting on the nervous Asaba's back as Reading hit the bottom of the table. Next up at Elm Park three days later were QPR, still a big enough name to bring Reading's floating punters out, but wrought by problems of their own. Over 10,000 came to see two sides desperate for a win.

I loved night games like those, the sky turning to pink and red over the Tilehurst End as the first half unfolds. We were in the deep, dark inside of the South Bank, a sea of anonymous heads straining to catch all the action. The floodlights bring out the colour of everything inside the ground and subdue, put into shadow, the daily townscape beyond. Reading piled forward and Lee Hodges stretched and nodded in a rebound after 10 minutes. The South Bank was in great voice, full of the raucous rudeness and vibrant insult the visit of a bigger name usually brings out. "You're not fit to wear our hoops" to the only other club that does so. We chanted for the dismissal of their manager before they could and told them they were so loud (about 2,000 of them) they sounded like Aldershot. Their full back, Brevett was hounded to distraction on account of his first name. "Rufus is a dog's name!" A second goal, a goal for Asaba, and Reading could relax and play and get all the goal-less frustration out of their system. Rangers were hanging in rags, arguing with each other. Hodges again, Robins twice, Andy Bernal all went close and missed. "Sweet Molly Malone". "Oh, what can it be?" Thunderous applause on the half-time whistle and out we shuffled into the smells of the bogs and the burger van.

Once the programme shop, now the police control room and refreshment kiosk.

45 minutes to a win and a rise of 10 places up the table. Another goal and we were there. But the surge had gone, the caution crept in. Even so, we looked okay until, in the 70th minute, a goof from our youngsters on the left led to a cross arcing in on to the unmarked head of their £2 million striker. 1-1 and panic stations. Two minutes later a frantic failure to clear from the other flank and a deflected own goal rolled over for 1-2. The crowd try to shout Reading back into it but the belief, the composure, has gone and the hoofing started. Asaba was taken off to general agreement but his replacement, local youngster Neville Roach, didn't see a good ball on which to stake his claim and the game faded away. We went home thinking 'we didn't deserve that'.

Fellow relegation candidates Oxford were the next visitors and by now Reading had no wins, one point and two goals from six games, were, obviously, bottom and enduring our worst ever start to the season. It was still a bit early to sack the new manager and his signings but lose this next one and where would we go?

Everything's going to be alright

In the vital local derby Oxford took a dodgy lead after two minutes. The chips were really down but Asaba at the far post headed an equaliser that neutralised the cynics on the terraces. In the second half Hodges stabbed home the winner. A tense crowd got right behind the team and cheered Reading home to their first win in a game of immense pressure. The following week a number of first half defensive lapses led to Tranmere taking a 5-0 half-time lead, 6-0 it finished, and John Madejski took Terry Bullivant for a walk and a talk on the Prenton Park pitch afterwards.

Something turned somewhere. A Peterborough player was sent off in the first minute and Reading reached the League Cup Third Round with a 2-0 away win. Then we won by the same score at Fratton Park. Promotion-chasing Sunderland came to Elm Park next and a fast and bold Asaba hit two first-half goals. To be fair, Reading had the rub of the green and scored twice more. Just before the end, a frustrated Sunderland fan scaled the fence at the Town End, seized a dead ball, lashed it into Steve Mautone's net and escaped into the terraces to laughs and cheers all round. On the back of two encouraging performances Reading were out of the relegation places and Asaba looked like he could play.

A week later, in an atmosphere reminiscent of the old Fourth Division – pouring rain, empty terraces, red-shirted Northern opposition – Crewe took a 3-0 lead in under half an hour. But Reading responded bringing the game back to 2-3 by half-time, 3-3 in the second half with the crowd singing "We're gonna win 4-3", and we almost did. Reading were defending better away from home with 3 successive 0-0s.

Sky's TV cameras came to Elm Park for the Friday night floodlit visit of champions-elect Nottingham Forest, as did the largest crowd of the season so far, over 12,500. Reading were looking beaten, 0-2 down in the second half, when the Forest keeper was controversially sent off and Martin Williams scored from the penalty. Forest quickly restored their two goal advantage but the crowd had scented blood and roared the team on as first James Lambert dribbled through for a brilliant individual goal and then Linvoy Primus headed the equaliser. But the glorious winner never came, 3-3 again. The noisy crowd sighed and went home half-satisfied that we had held our own with the top team.

Though Darius Wdowczyk and Steve Mautone were now also lost to injury there was a feeling that the team was beginning to gel. Ray Houghton and James Lambert were playing well, Martin Williams had a good understanding with 7 goal Asaba and

Caskey and Morley were returning to fitness. Supporters were seeing the shape of the team emerge and, conscious of the coming of the end of Elm Park, enjoying the last few months on the terraces. The vocal support and the mood was upbeat. At the end of October Reading lay an improving 19th in the table and had booked a place in the 4th Round of the League Cup. Meanwhile at Smallmead the West Stand steel structure was up and the new pitch was being seeded.

The back of Norfolk Road where Reading played once.

The front of Norfolk Road where Reading played ever since.

Sitting on the ledge of the bank.

Reading Heaven Wolves Hell

One wouldn't expect a similar book about Wolves to deal in detail with matches against Reading nor do we have any particular animus against the Old Gold and Black Country Wanderers. It was simply matters of circumstance, character and co-incidence that almost every visit by Wolves has been some kind of defining moment in Reading's recent history. (Wolves were decent enough to recognise this and, for Elm Park's final game, sent a tongue-in-cheek message that read, *"...Never again to play at Elm Park. We are, of course, distraught!"* So, it was not a surprise, having disposed of one ex-manager, Jimmy Quinn now playing for Peterborough, in the 2nd Round of the League Cup, that we should draw the beleaguered Mark McGhee's Wolves in the Third Round. There was, shall we say, some history to this fixture.

Wolves first post-war visit to Elm Park had been in the Second Round of the same competition in 1978. They came as a First Division club to us, a Fourth Division club and were well-beaten 1-0 on a night marred by some crowd violence. Their manager, Sammy Chung, an ex-Reading player, lost his job shortly afterwards.

Yet, when the clubs next met 7 years later in Division Three, there could have been no hotter favourite to win a single football match than Reading. It was our 14th game of the season and we had won the previous 13, breaking the all-time record for the best start to a season. Our team was in that blessed mental state that comes once a sporting lifetime, if you are lucky, of believing they were invincible, no matter what fate or the ref held in store. By contrast, Wolves were a patched together side, bottom of the table, in total financial turmoil and followed by fans angrily protesting against their absentee board of directors. At stake was Reading's opportunity to lay a shared claim on the all-time 14 successive League wins at any point in the season and to break it by the end of the week.

Elm Park's capacity had been reduced to 8,000 following the post-Bradford Fire restrictions and some fans had been locked out of the previous game. Clearance had been achieved for a larger capacity, some said 11,500, but thousands more swarmed ticketless, for there were none issued, down the Tilehurst and Oxford Roads to see this all-conquering team make history and none were gainsaid at the gates. It was the last very big game of the 'just turn up and get in' era, when blokes in factories, offices and pubs all over the town and county said, "Come on, let's go". And go they did, like iron filings drawn to the magnet of football history in the making. The record books say 13,465 but the noise and pressure inside said more as, remarkably for that era, home and away fans happily shared the non-segregated Town End.

Boot Room.

Changing Rooms.

The South Bank broadside.

Years later, the former managing director Mike Lewis said there were 17,500 inside. Trevor Senior recalled, "the crowd was unbelievable, biggest I played in front of at Elm Park. The South Bank was packed with all these little dots of people willing you to get that win. It was a lovely night for football".

On a calm October evening Wolves scored early. Reading had the play but no goals at half-time. There was no immediate breakthrough in the second half either, then Kevin Bremner stretched for a long cross and savagely volleyed into the corner of the Tilehurst End goal. The doors were down now and Reading piled in, to huge roars from the packed crowd. Senior bagged the second then missed a third and, with the match won and our head of steam gone, Wolves broke to score again five minutes from the end. Despite the disappointment of the end of the winning run, the crowd gave the players a tumultous ovation (reasonable enough as we were 14 points clear before the end of October!) Reading went up as Champions and Wolves went down to the Fourth for the first time.

They returned in 1988/89 on their way to the Third Division championship, beating us soundly 2-0 at Elm Park, in a match that does not really trouble the memory. We caught up with them after our promotion to Division One (as Division Two had now become) and opened the season at Molineux losing very unluckily 1-0. With both teams challenging at the top, ITV covered the return on a damp and claggy Sunday afternoon in December 1994. It was Reading's first game after McGhee and his management team had left to join Leicester City. Supporters were furious over this loss and fearful that all the good work, with Reading now in their highest League position of all time, would be undone. Wolves were full of big name players and managed by recently-deposed England boss Graham Taylor. One fellow in C Stand took the trouble of reminding him of his recent previous predicament by placing a turnip above his head on the perspex top of the dug-out. Again Wolves scored early but the resolve of our players and our crowd together was as good as I ever saw at Elm Park. In a hard, full-throated game Reading came back to lead 2-1, were drawn back to 2-2, took the lead again and finally resolved the result in the last minute. 4-2 to Reading, and a message to the world that the show goes on. And it did, past Wolves defeated by Bolton in the play-off semi-finals, all the way to Wembley but sadly not beyond.

Both sides struggled the following season. McGhee had left Leicester to become Wolves manager by the time the fixture came round, Reading's last home game of the season and one we needed to win to stay up. It was as tense as a cup final at the start. Reading took an early lead and finished with a magical goal from Quinn to win 3-0. Wolves were poor and the Reading fans exultant.

Bogs.

Burgers.

"Did you SEE that ?"

Outside the ground the frustrated Wolves fans again sang "shit ground, no fans" but that just added to the pleasure.

Another season, another year later, Reading safe but nothing more, McGhee's Wolves closing in on their Premiership grail. By now it had got personal, got too much between McGhee and many Reading fans ("the 300 guys under the shed" he once intemperately said of our loyal support). There were three ex-Reading players in his team and he had already taken a fourth to Leicester. In a rough game, on a hard pitch on a bright afternoon in front of a full house, Wolves knocked in an iffy goal 15 minutes from time. Time was up as Reading crossed from the right and a back-header found Archie Lovell in all the space he needed to equalise. And if that were not enough, on top of the crashing noise of the "Oh, what can it be" song ringing around the ground, a few moments later Lovell found himself jiggling the ball in the penalty area before sliding it home for the winner. Like an AREFF cartoon of old, the ground seemed to bounce and explode. 'Little' Reading were vindicated! 'Big' Wolves missed promotion.

This series of matches came to matter something special for Reading fans and, consequently, something hellish for Wolves supporters. It created a rivalry for the first time with a 'big' club - the club of Major Buckley, Billy Wright, Fifties floodlit world-beaters - where Reading always came out on top. It told people to think again about the status of Reading Football Club and the football world did take note of Reading-Wolves games.

And so six months later, in Elm Park's final season, in the 1997/98 League Cup, Reading – newly on the up – meet a Wolves on the slide and a McGhee shadowed by the prospect of dismissal. It was a rainy night and a skiddy top. The Wolves fans were thin on the terrace. 'That' song boomed out again as the game kicked off with Reading attacking the Town End as usual. It was a messy, tense start with plenty of chances. After half an hour Michael Meaker crossed from the right and at the far post Wolves centre-half (and former Reading captain!) Williams turned it into his own net. "Oh, Adie, Adie. Adie, Adie, Adie Williams," sang the South Bank joyfully as in by-gone days. Two minutes later Phil Parkinson ran through the curtain of rain swirling the pitch, pushing team-mate Houghton of out his way as he went, and drove into the top corner from 25 yards. "AAAAAHH!" "You're gonna get the sack, you're gonna get the sack, and now you've gotta believe us, you're get the sack." Bull scored for Wolves but at the start of the second Lambert and Asaba ripped their defence to shreds as first Meaker and then Keith McPherson stretched the lead to 4-1. Reading were on fire, Wolves were in utter disarray and the crowd weren't slow to tell McGhee. Wolves came back towards the end and it finished 4-2. The tannoy announced the Tilehurst slope would be closed after the match (a euphemism that the police were alert to the possibility of post-match trouble) but, for the Reading faithful, the result itself was redemption enough. The crowd left the ground chanting "Sack McGhee, Sack McGhee", when once the cry was "Mark McGhee, Mark McGhee". Afterwards, while McGhee was still locked with his players and directors in the dressing room, Terry Bullivant said on TV, in that deadpan way of his, "Elm Park's a great place especially in the evenings".

Christmas and Cup Glory

In the League, November brought two wins, one draw and three defeats. Morley and Caskey were restored to regular duty at the expense of Meaker and Houghton and the football got gritty. The result of the month came in the League Cup where Reading came from 1-2 behind to win 3-2 at Premiership Leeds United in the surprise of the Fourth Round. Asaba, Williams and Morley all scored and chairman John Madejski was happily quoted as saying, "that shows what they are capable of".

Yet three days later, on a soft damp Elm Park afternoon, Reading got off to a sleepy start against Ipswich and were comprehensively beaten 0-4. Cup success and a move out of the relegation places had created a few lazy minds and casual bodies. But, as they had been doing for three seasons, Reading bounced straight back with a win at Stoke and then a home victory in a tiring, hard-fought game against Charlton. Wolves were the next visitors and another bloody battle ensued. But, apart from the period around a couple of sendings-off, the game never took off like the fixture usually did. Perhaps we were now sated with victory?

Elm Park's last live TV appearance came at midday on Boxing Day and, despite the inconvenience of the kick-off time, over 10,000 saw Reading take an early two goal lead over West Bromwich and hang on 2-1. At the half-way point in Elm Park's last season, Reading lay 18th in Division One, with a home tie in the League Cup Quarter-finals and an away tie at non-League opposition in the FA Cup to come. Winger Jason Bowen and centre half Gareth Davies had been bought to strengthen a squad now lacking Mautone, Meaker, Hunter, Wdowczyk, McPherson and Primus (the centre-back partnership that had seen us through the first 20 games together) and had Houghton and Lovell not fully fit. Nonetheless, the prospects seemed fair at this point in time. The first game of the New Year was the Quarter-final on 6th January against Middlesbrough, a very strong Division One team. The tie would be decided at Elm Park on the night after extra-time and penalties if necessary.

This was only the second Cup Quarter-final held at Elm Park. And, as with that 1901 clash with Spurs, this one was determined by the referee too. It was a cold, wet, wet night and an all-ticket crowd of 13,000, tense and making less noise than usual. It was a tight game with the bigger, stronger visitors making the better chances, though Morley missed the type of header he often scored with in the second half. With extra-time looming Boro were denied by a questionable off-side decision.

Hustle.

Bustle.

Perfect pitch for the League Cup-tie.

Then, right at the death, with spats between players breaking out around the pitch and others lying injured, there was a pause. On the restart it appeared to all as if Reading had the free kick on the half-way line and players moved up to take attacking positions. But suddenly the ref's indication changed. Boro's ball! Three deft touches later it was in the corner of Reading's thinly guarded net and no amount of protest about the incompetence and injustice of it made any difference. One stirring last effort was in vain and the final whistle went to angry chants of "1-0 to the referee". We might not have been the better side, we might not have won in extra-time on penalties but we felt we deserved the chance to see, one last chance to get a really big game - like a League Cup Semi-Final against Liverpool live on ITV, in Elm Park's last season - and it was denied.

It was a physically and emotionally draining night but over the next four weeks Reading would play 9 matches, five of them cup-ties, on hard winter pitches. In the final analysis this was probably what did for Bullivant and his team.

Relegation rivals Bury snatched two points away from Reading with a late, undeserved and carelessly given equaliser on a quiet and dank afternoon. In midweek, Morley scraped a draw from a possible ignominy on a quagmire at Cheltenham. On the Saturday, local lads Lovell and Lambert lashed in their last goals for the club as Reading won the return derby against Swindon very easily. Nicky Hammond was heard to suggest afterwards on TV that we were "not far off a play-off place". 10 days later, the 4-1 defeat at Bradford City was a precursor of the reality around the corner. Reading lacked heart and fitness. Paul Bodin and Michael Thorp from the Reserves were thrown into central defence in a struggling team.

In the meantime Reading edged Cheltenham out of Cup 2-1 in the replay and then hung on for another replay with a draw at Cardiff. Though a strong Birmingham team was 2-0 beaten at Elm Park it was only after they had reduced themselves to 9 men through their own aggression. Cardiff clearly fancied their chances in the Cup replay and brought a large following. Pubs in the town centre were smashed, 29 arrests made after clashes in the town, and in the ground a female steward was assaulted. "These were scenes we hoped had disappeared", said the club. It was a nasty throwback to the 70s and early 80s, the last really dangerous and disorderly atmosphere at Elm Park, when fear was in the air and fans had to work out the safest route home through the car-jammed and crowd-darkened back streets.

The pitch was frost-bound and got worse as the long night went on. Cardiff took a first half breakaway lead and Reading looked to be struggling to get it back against opposition from two divisions below.

Into the melting pot.

A win on the night would put us in the Fifth Round for the first time since 1935 after a series of Fourth Round embarrassments down the years. Morley equalised with a header, his last goal for the club. Extra-time was scoreless so Reading came to their first FA Cup penalty shoot-out. The referee took the players to the Tilehurst End, where 10 years earlier Michael Gilkes' penalty shoot-out winner took Reading to Wembley for the first time in the Simod Cup Final, and 53 years earlier Arsenal's Cliff Bastin put us out of the 5th Round for the last time. Victory or shame beckoned on a raw and angry night. Two up in the shoot-out Reading allowed Cardiff to draw level before the final heroic save from the stomach-strained Hammond was greeted by the roar of the crowd and the air turned white with the bellowing of frosty breath. The party was over and the sirens began to wail again.

Penalty shoot-out.

Yesss !!!

Take your places for the last floodlit match.

Avalanche

Three days after the maelstrom of the Cup replay, Tranmere Rovers came, without a goal in 8 games. Police sticky tape covered the crush barriers in the corner of the Town End near the South Bank keeping a few hundred docile travellers at bay whilst shrieking to the world 'the horse has bolted'. Replacing the hero Hammond in goal was third choice keeper Sal Bibbo making what turned out to be his sixth and penultimate League appearance. This was already Reading's 41st game of the season. It was a cold, grey afternoon with just 7,000 present and it felt like the calm, old Third Division.

In the 8th minute Bibbo punched a ball he should have caught and Tranmere picked it up and ended their goal famine. The first pebble. Then Tranmere broke and scored from a Reading free-kick on the edge of their own area. And the next pebble rolled in the avalanche of misery that was to engulf Reading Football Club. The team were tired and dismal, so poor they were booed off the pitch, 1-3 losers. The Cup-run fizzled out in the obscurity of a Friday night at Bramall Lane, Reading conceding in the last minute, not having managed a shot all game. The fixture was played on Friday rather than Sunday to rest the players before the game at Sunderland on the Tuesday. A 4-1 hiding suggested it made little difference. Andy Bernal had now succumbed to injury and Andy Legg was bought from Birmingham to replace Steve Swales at left back.

Next at Elm Park were Portsmouth, left abject and ruined by the Terry Venables regime, but now calling on Alan Ball to revive their spirits. They had won a game the week before so the result could be the beginning of a run for them or the end of a blip. It was a dull, hard, muddy, tense struggle, an obvious 0-0 in the making. Except that a badly-struck free kick hit one Pompey man on the leg and fell to another to sweep home. For the first time in months I could smell relegation in the ground.

Three days later, another big name struggler, Manchester City, appeared for what was the final competitive match under the Elm Park floodlights. As with Wolves, we had something on City now and we survived a couple of early scares. Then Hodges and Houghton scored in quick succession, the game was won and most of the 11,500 crowd went home happy after another great Elm Park night. In the dressing room there were more casualties: a broken finger for Hammond and injuries for Parkinson and Hodges that would put them out for the season. (Parkinson was back in three weeks, Hodges missed the next season as well).

The Tilehurst Road.

Sentries.

Nice ground, no fans.

A new keeper, Nicky Colgan of Chelsea, was brought in on loan for the game at Crewe, made a match-losing schoolboy error on 10 minutes and conceded 15 more in the next 4 games as Reading simply fell under the rocks of misfortune.

A combination of the half-fit, the disheartened and the on loan lost 1-5 at Stockport in midweek before yet another vital home game against bottom of the table Port Vale. By now the need to turn the tide was very clear to the players and the public. Despite overcoming his disastrous start, Bullivant had not won the approval of the supporters. The tactics and pattern of play seemed to change too frequently, substitutes were under-employed and the same heart for the contest was not present in all games.

It was a crunch match on a dry and bumpy pitch and Port Vale won easily by 3-0 with the first goal a gift from Reading. At half-time part of the South Bank was chanting "Terry Bullivant's blue-and-white army" and part was chanting "Bullivant out". By the end it was obvious the crowd wanted a word with the club and was going to invade the pitch to do so. A lone female was first to sit on the centre spot and was swiftly joined by several hundred more fans before, as had become customary, they marched on the main stand and surrounded the directors box chanting "Bullivant out". On the previous such occasion 18 months earlier ("Quinn out") Uri Geller, using a megaphone, had interceded on behalf of the chairman but this time Madejski stood on his own, looking stony-faced into the crowd. The invaders were on his side but against his manager. They keenly feared relegation at just the moment Reading were due to leap forward to a new stadium. They sung "nice ground, no fans" – a pithy and pointed message. I looked at the chairman looking silently at the supporters below, wondering what was going through his mind. Call the riot police? Sack the manager tomorrow? Sell the club? At last, he was found a microphone and spoke, reassuring all of his commitment to the club and pledging to do whatever it took to turn the business round. The people had had a signal from the leader and left.

And so too did John Madejski. He never saw another match at Elm Park. What must have been going through his mind was, how do I sort all this out before I leave the country for a year in a few days time? More efforts were made in the transfer market but no one would come, a sports psychologist was employed to help the players and team changes were made. Booty, Bowen, Asaba and McPherson were all to see virtually no more action for the rest of the season. The performance at Sheffield United was credited as an improvement although the game was lost 0-4. Nine games to go and the next was at Oxford, another poorly-regarded side.

John Madejski (far right) faces the fans.

The Reading support at the Cuckoo Lane end was large and feisty, seeking a shock victory or acrid showdown. In the first half we barely had a chance, Davies went missing again near half-time and they scored through the hole. In the second half Oxford attacked the end at which the Reading support was stood and soon scored twice more. The Reading keeper, Colgan, was injured and hopping on one leg but getting little sympathy from his team-mates. It had become an excruciating farce and the Reading end, which had supported well enough when the outcome was in the balance, turned on its team – "You're not fit to wear the hoops"- and its manager "Terry, Terry, what's the score?" I looked at Ray Houghton as he walked off: he was staring, glassy-eyed, stunned. The rest came off, each alone, and that night I believe, mentally at least, we were relegated. After the game Reading fans, besieged dressing rooms and the team coach was impeded.

The following afternoon, despite the board's protestations, Terry Bullivant resigned. He said he "could get no more out of the players" and was fed-up with "the mickey-taking". He had never struck up any relationship with the fans for whom he was 'Terry the Taxi'. Neither he nor his assistant ever appeared at any functions for ordinary supporters. His downbeat style and lack of fame did not help and neither did the fact that 11 of his 38 League games were lost by three goals or more. On the other hand, in the 23 League games from 13th September to the end of January, exactly half a League season between the rushed start and the injury crisis, Reading won 9, drew 8 and lost 6. That kind of playing record over a whole season would have meant 8th place! However, in six weeks, Reading lost 9 out of 10 games, Bullivant his managerial career and, effectively, the club its First Division place. The one-line verdict on Bullivant was 'Decent bloke but out of his depth'.

With Madejski out of the country and Bullivant gone, Chief Executive Nigel Howe and Reserves team manager Alan Pardew were left to issue the rallying cries. 8,500 turned up to see yet another struggler, Huddersfield Town. Unknown to almost all, the Newcastle coach Tommy Burns was among those on a passionate South Bank. Colgan was shot (not literally!) so the still-injured Hammond was pressed back into service between the posts, metaphorically the one-armed replacing the one-legged. The spirit was there but the luck and the finishing were not. Near the end of a game we could have won, Hammond was unable to get down to make an easy save and it finished 0-2. There was generous applause for the players and Pardew at the final whistle and that was pretty much the funeral for that Reading team. It was to be no more. But if all the Cup games had counted for League points instead we would have been safe by a mile. If…

Tommy Burns, the new man.

Tommy Burns and the Magnificent Seven

The Reading board needed a manager fast and in the two days between Bullivant's resignation and the Huddersfield game must have re-contacted Tommy Burns who had turned the job down the previous year. This time Burns signed up and made the right gung-ho noises about "7 games to save the Royals". One of his first acts was to meet with the rank and file supporters one weekday evening. Over five hundred stood on the South Bank to listen to his plans.

Another was to break the all-time record for most signings on transfer deadline day. By close of business £760,000 had been spent on six players and another taken on loan. All had Scottish or Newcastle backgrounds, one goalkeeper, one centre half, two midfielders and three forwards. "It's like a Tartan Army down here", said one. Burns revealed that there were only 12 fit players at the club when he arrived. Several had played with injuries and were now to be rested. The 13 picked to play at Ipswich showed 8 changes from the last match. With renewed hope, a large Reading contingent travelled to Suffolk. Bernal and Legg were sent off, rather harshly, and an unlucky 1-0 defeat ensued. There were six games to go, three against the sides about to be promoted. It was all over bar a miracle.

Burns first home game was against Stoke, who were in as bad a state as Reading, and played worse on the day. 10,500 welcomed Burns and five of the magnificent seven, and saw Reading win 2-0 and score for the last time at Elm Park. Afterwards one felt the Evening Post might be overplaying the 'magnificent' tag but Tommy Burns was saying all the right things about 'professionalism' and 'big club' and 'training morning and afternoon'.

A predictable defeat at Charlton materialised and now it was a question of when, and not if, we dropped. On Easter Monday, Middlesbrough, close to an automatic promotion place, returned. Now they had the legendary enigma of Paul Gascoigne in their ranks, a man seeking to seal a berth in England's World Cup finals squad for the summer. It was a typical bright sunny Bank Holiday and thousands of casuals and star-seekers turned out. The gates for the home terraces were shut early, to much complaint from late-arriving regulars, some of whom insinuated themselves on to the away end. It was exactly this kind of fixture for which the new stadium was being built, its vast seated capacity able to absorb thousands of walk-up casual punters at £14 a throw rather than tell them to get there early or send them away sore and frustrated. Inside, Boro scored early and their applecart looked fairly safe for the duration. Gazza played a pretty hour's worth before being subbed and the crowd seemed resigned to a drama-less relegation.

The back of B stand.

"Bovril, please, love".

Time runs out for Reading against Boro.

It was not to be sealed at Wolves of all places, thankfully, but in the last minute of the match the following week that simultaneously promoted Nottingham Forest. Bart-Williams scored the late winner. Minutes before, with the score 0-0, Paul Brayson hit the post. It was that sort of season. McGhee was decent enough in victory at Molineux and inelegantly put his finger on the central playing issue in after-match interview. "Reading were out-physicalled today by younger, stronger players." To be fair, the rescue by the magnificent seven was never really on. They were the players that were available to buy, fitter but no better than those they replaced. If by luck they had geiled straight away we would still have needed four wins right against the form book in the last seven games.

Across the world, John Madejski generously shouldered the blame. "We are a small club, we can't match the machinations of clubs like Middlesbrough... Sadly we haven't been able to make football pay at Elm Park." Nearer to home Jimmy Quinn claimed that he would have kept Reading up, while the spurned superfan Uri Geller felt, "I believed I helped them psychically. The day I left they went down and down and are now relegated". Fans wondered whether any Division Two club would need a stadium with 24,000 seats.

Relegation made the final home game against Norwich, already sold-out, irrelevant in terms of the result but still of great consequence as an occasion on which to say goodbye to Elm Park, a whole era, a way of football life. The team that began the season had died, the ground was about to die and so too inevitably was something about our club itself.

Last Rites.

When Did You Last See Elm Park?

Until the start of 1997/98 we had been able to put the idea of Elm Park closing into the distant future. But come August it was the last season, the last first game of the season, the last this and that and all the finalities hung like a pall of sorrows to come over the whole season. Like several other fans I know I paid my last respects to various parts of the ground, watching matches from all four sides. On the Town End, amid the Huddersfield fans, I came across another old schoolmate standing where, he, his father and his grandfather always used to stand before it was made the away end in the early 1980s. His father packed in going when that happened. It must have been well over thirty years since I had seen a first team game there, since I left my cardigan on the front wall (if it had been graffiti it would still have been there!).

I spent a couple of jacketed and wrapped midwinter afternoons on the Tilehurst End, where the accents always seem more Berrrkshire. I rediscovered the 'secret passage' that led down from the back of the terrace that I knew as a child playing here but had since forgotten. You could sense the closeness of the players and, together with the relative quietness around, it put me in mind of my own footballing days in nearby Prospect Park.

But I was always going to watch the final game from my old place at the back of the South Bank just to the right of the half-way line, to take in that letterbox view for the countless and last time. Stood there in a group of a dozen mates, who I'd known half my life or longer, been to so many matches with and played in so many games with.

Norwich City were the opponents for the last League match. The fixture was actively marketed as the farewell to Elm Park and some people flew from Australia to be there. One was a kid I had sat next to at Wilson School 30 odd years ago and the programme announced him now to be a Reverend. He must have seen from the programme that I'm still following the team too, and so football helps binds our knowledge of our old community!

I had often wondered what it would be like and how I would feel leaving the ground for the last time. Of course, what I wanted was some tumultous, victorious finish in the last ten minutes and then, with thousands of others, to come on the pitch, to wander about the ground savouring the last moments as the life of the place drained away into the quietening evening air. When the magic of the players and the specialness of the stadium had disappeared the crowd would sweep forward like the sea to reclaim the place made noble by football deeds and turn it to ordinary Reading clay once more.

Help yourself.

But if you were there you know it did not happen like that. On the South Bank before the game we had sung the names of old heroes, Trevor Senior, Shaka Hislop, Adie Williams and anyone else those under 25 could remember but nothing else good can I recall from the day. The kick-off was an untimely 1.30pm on a Sunday, fans were instructed not to bring cameras or then, if they must, disposables only, an inappropriate programme of events was offered (lap of honour!) and not delivered, the match was of numbing dullness and lost without a final, defiant huzzah and then there was nothing. What I wanted was a definite point at which we, the supporters, said or sung goodbye to our ground. The crowd, unfulfilled yet emotional, were waiting but the club appeared broken and leaderless. The only voice to be heard was that of the safety officer imploring people to get off the pitch. While the police dogs faced the turf-throwing fans, his siren droned over an angry crowd, held back reclaiming this place that was special to them because it was needed for a tournament involving some local businesses the following week. When it was clear nothing was going to be rescued from the afternoon we left numb and frustrated, no tears, nothing but quiet fury.

An hour or so later, it would be about 5pm now, the proper time to finish a match, a ground, a club, I went back to see what was going on. Michael Meaker, the last Reading player to score at Elm Park, looking showerfresh and carefree, was getting into his BMW convertible. You're not feeling what I'm feeling, I felt. I peered through the gates of the South Bank and saw some people on the pitch larking about so I drove round to the front. I was going to do something I always wanted to but never had done. I took a plastic ball out of my car and marched briskly up the B Stand steps and down the other side to the pitch, which was pretty well deserted now. Straight out on to the pitch, a couple of kids already in my tow, I took the ball and booted it into the Town End goal. Yes! And again for good measure. Yes! I could hear Fred Neate down the other end of the pitch yelling at whoever it was to clear off. I'd done what I wanted, scored a small point of retribution so I left the ball and the ground.

I was conscious of the symmetry, the fact that my first memory of Elm Park as a lost 5 year-old was being told to 'get out of it' and here now, after half a lifetime of devotion, it was much the same thing. And that would be have been a good enough ending, a storybook ending, a horror story.

But that was not the end. Elm Park stood for several more months and, for myself and many others, a valuable healing process took place before the bulldozers went in. I lost count of the number of final matches as Elm Park gently slipped away.

Rusting shabbiness.

Jostling darkness.

The Day of the Triffids ?

The ground was maintained over the summer just in case the Madejski Stadium was not completed on time and, on July 15th, Sheffield Wednesday visited for a pre-season friendly and were soundly beaten 3-0 on a lovely gentle summer's evening in front of a crowd of 7,500.

Thinking it was all over now, some idiots spoilt the occasion by breaking both crossbars (oh, it's finished with, so we might as well smash it now), thus giving the club some comfort for the way they had handled the Norwich game.

Still to come, however, and arranged at short notice as if tying up the loose ends of our Elm Park existence, were testimonials for Fred Neate and Michael Gilkes. Fred's, sadly for he deserved far better, was a low-key midweek match against a collection of redoubtable veterans. Whilst the guest list was a Who's Who of Reading football of the 50s and 60s there were few in the crowd to whom their names meant much. Few in the crowd at all if truth be told, less than 2,000, but at least the old names and old contributions were recognised in the old place for the last time.

And finally, but for the subsequent Barnet reserve match for which a couple of hundred die-hards gave up a Monday lunchtime, Gilkesy brought along the 1993-95 team under the management of the man many had been so upset by, Mark McGhee. McGhee, thankfully, was forgiven for the afternoon and welcomed warmly as were all those great names from the very recent glorious past. After 30 seconds it was, "Shaka, Shaka what's the score" and the big man held up two zeroes and everyone laughed. Gilkes crossed for Jimmy Quinn to score the first, just like old times, and then faded away, just like old times. But he tucked away a penalty before the end. Phil Parkinson played for the Gilkes' team and set about proving a point. The spindly goalposts had to be borrowed from Henley Town and the two ends were shut to save costs and we were mostly cheering a team we knew better and loved more than those now playing for Reading Football Club! It was dreamy stuff, an afternoon of reconciliation and happy endings for the 5,000 there.

And, for me, that still was not the end, even though by now the weeds were breaking through the Tilehurst End terracing. Chris Whalley, the Community Officer, arranged an over-35s tournament on the Friday before the contents of the ground were to be auctioned. The Supporters Club put in a team and I got to play on Elm Park for the first time. Okay, it was only 8-a-side and across the pitch, but it was good just to be out there, to sense how square the pitch felt, how raised it seemed when you looked towards the Town End and the houses sunken down in Norfolk Road, to run down the wing in front of the South Bank.

Signing off.

The dressing rooms were out of bounds so we changed in the executive boxes. There we met a silver-haired fellow in his 60s with that well-defined look of the ex-pro. "Yes, I've played a bit", he admitted, he being Johnny Brooks, formerly of Chelsea, Tottenham and England. Still could too. And, in another team John Gorman, the assistant England coach, and Mike Kearney, mine host at the Rendezvous and an ex-Reading centre-forward. It was a great evening, football for pleasure's sake.

The power to the floodlights was cut so we could only play until the light went and, of course, we had never seen football in the dusk at Elm Park. It was eerie, it gave a real sense of the night falling forever. With a friend from Wilson School days in my team, it brought back memories of us playing together in such fading light, thirty years ago in Brock Barracks or Prospect Park, never then presuming to think we would play on Elm Park itself or that it would ever be knocked down. In near darkness we changed and left a living Elm Park for the last time, as players ourselves now, for a final pint in the Rendezvous. I felt sad but okay, complete, about it now.

Two days later the club auctioned off the contents of Elm Park. In order not to spoil my current last memories by witnessing the bids for, say, Lot 390 – the carpet-tiles from the Vice Presidents Lounge, I stayed at home. Thereafter Elm Park was a wreck in the process of demolition and I visited it, as did so many others, on that basis only until there was nothing left but the back wall of the Town End toilets, topped with that luxuriant growth.

So when did I last see Elm Park? I wouldn't pick any of these moments. I'd pick a time when it was still at its typical, earthy, up yours, vibrant best, with surfaces everywhere glistening in the rain and floodlight shine, a sticky wet top, a raucous packed crowd whose noise bounces back off the South Bank roof, an opposition who fancied themselves at the start crumbling in the face of our powerful play and a terrific last minute goal to send us all off to a nice West Reading pub in good spirits. And that was the last floodlit match at Elm Park, a 3-0 win against Manchester City in February, the last time I left the place with footballing hope in my heart, little though I knew that at the time.

One end.

Another.

One end.

Another.

PART THREE   **THE FIRST SEASON**

Laying the foundations.

From the mud and dust outside Courage's brewery.

The Building of the Madejski Stadium

It takes a long time to build a football stadium. It's not so much the building that takes the time as getting the permission to build and get road access and the finance to make the scheme stand up. In fact, the Madejski Stadium was built in only 14 months from start to finish, compared with, say, 31 years for the Elm Park we knew (1926-57).

Following the discussions initiated by the council in 1992 it became clear, if it were not already, that Reading Football Club was the only 'player' with funds enough to make the 'Smallmead scheme' fly. The ideas of the ice-rink, the baseball, the tennis centre came to nothing. Over the course of 1993 discussions between the council and the club continued to the point when, on 9th December 1993, the council revealed its plans to open up the Smallmead area with the extension of the A33 Relief Road. This made possible the £200 million Reading Business Park development by the Prudential on land adjacent to the M4. At this stage it was not clear exactly where a sports stadium would be sited. The initial thought was to place it to the north and west of the speedway stadium, effectively behind it from the view of the relief road. By April 1995 it was clear that a second, larger and more prominent site – where the stadium now stands – was under consideration.

The Royals for once were fortunate with the timing. When discussions began in 1992 the average crowd was only 4,000 and the projected size of the stadium 15,000. By the time decisions had to be made, Reading were on the verge of the Premier-ship and the football boom was continuing. Consequently the stadium capacity was upped to 25,000 when publicly revealed in August 1995. Even so, at the time this was seen as a massive leap of faith in the future of the club. Few fans expected a new ground of this size and the Evening Post described it as "Reading's Dream Home". Nigel Howe was hired to manage the project and soon became Chief Executive of the club. Costs were expected to be £25-30 million and the opening date was set as August 1997. Anyone who has ever employed a builder will not be surprised to know it took 50% longer and cost 50% more to complete – and did not quite match the original plans! But anyone who takes such early planning statements at face value does not live in the real world.

Within months the club was holding meetings with fans and local residents and showing a scale model of the stadium complex. Howe claimed the ground would match any in the country. "Make no mistake, it will be a spectacular design with state-of-the-art facilities. One of the most important aspects is that it will be a seven-day-a-week operation. Apart from Wembley there will be the largest number of car parking spaces at a stadium in the country.

The West Stand seen from where the East Stand will go.

We aim to use this area to the full and there is the possibility of staging concerts." The possibility of ground-sharing with Reading Rugby Club had also been mentioned. He continued, "Elm Park is not a nice place to go and watch a football match for a number of reasons, not least the lack of comfort and the abysmal car parking arrangements. We believe a lot of people would go to a game if they knew the facilities were good and the ground accessible". At the same time, plans were revealed to flatten Elm Park and build 128 dwellings there. According to these plans the Royals Rendezvous would be retained.

By August 1996 detailed plans of the stadium were published, describing it as a unique construction for this country, the only similar examples being in Italy and the USA. The opening date had been put back to December 1997 because of the huge amount of legal work required to complete the deal between the many different parties. In funding terms there was now a shortfall of £10 million that John Madejski was seeking to raise. "It's been a struggle pulling the deal together but it's important everything is done properly. There's no point going for a quick fix. We must have a stadium that people are proud of," he said. "I still don't think people have grasped the importance or the size of this project. It's enormous". Meanwhile Reading kicked off the 1996/97 season with a 1-0 win over Sheffield United in a boiling hot Elm Park, crammed with 11,000 fans. Three miles away to the south the scrubby, bushy land of Smallmead was far out of most minds and sights.

By November there was further news of delay owing to the lack of resolution of the legal issues affecting the Smallmead site. The date for the move was put back to August 1998 and the car park was down from 3,000 to 2,000 spaces. The club were still searching for a major sponsor who would have ground-naming rights, as in the Reebok Stadium at Bolton.

Finally, at the FA headquarters in Lancaster Gate, the legal agreements were signed on 29th April 1997. It was simultaneously announced that John Madejski was funding the £10 million shortfall in funds and that the ground would be called the Madejski Stadium. It was, he later said, "not my idea. I hope I haven't offended too many people. I feel a little ambivalent about the fact". A new badge, or logo, for the Royals was also revealed to coincide with the move. Player-manager Jimmy Quinn expressed the view that the new stadium would be an asset in attracting more talented players to the club. On 2nd June 1997 John Madejski, spade in hand, performed the ground-turning ceremony and work to clear the site of waste and pollution began.

Supporters, sceptical by nature, were now convinced the move was going to happen. (At nearby Oxford United they had been talking about leaving The Manor for over 30 years.) Fans had played very little part in the debate and the plans.

John Madejski in the Directors Box.

There were a couple of minor fan-based schemes to raise funds in support of the new venture but the money amassed was inconsequential in the face of the scale of the project. The figure of £37 million was the one most commonly and blithely batted around in the media. Not the sort of stuff you could collect in a bucket or on a blanket or from a raffle. Over a decade either side of the war a strong Supporters' Club contributed about £1 million, in today's money, to ground development at Elm Park that made a real difference. In today's society, where we are so much more conscious of the needs of those in other countries, fund-raising from the public on that kind of level is no longer conceivable. As for multiplying it by 37 and dividing the time to collect it in half.... The costs of the Madejski Stadium were in a different league and the money that paid the bills almost intangible, inconceivable to the average supporter.

From press reports we know that almost £3 million came from the Football Trust and, it was rumoured, that just over £4 million came from the sale of the Elm Park site to Barratts. I don't think the club had any 'piggy bank' savings nor were players sold to finance the development. Madejski himself guaranteed the £10 million shortfall which leaves just £20 million to account for. Nigel Howe, quoted in the Evening Post, said "most of the money will come from the leasing of the land to non-food retail outlets … and various sponsorships". In time, an enormous B&Q hardware store emerged at the base of the stadium, alongside Comet and Allied Carpets, and the names Hewlett-Packard and Panasonic were liberally affixed to two of the stands.

Equally, it was not immediately transparent as to what elements comprised the £37 million project cost. The land itself was sold to the club for £1 but came with a bill for de-toxification of £6 million (some reports say £10 million). Reading Football Club had to contribute to the building of the Relief Road; one report said £6 million. The conference centre and banqueting facilities would have involved additional costs that make comparisons with other stadia difficult. Huddersfield Town's internationally acclaimed, but initially three-sided, McAlpine Stadium came in at around £16 million. It seems likely that the football venue part of the Madejski Stadium would have cost upwards of £20 million. In the Report and Accounts for 1998 a figure of almost £24 million is given for 'fixed assets under construction'. On that basis the Madejski Stadium is worth 6 times as much as a to-be-flattened Elm Park realised in sale. It is a massive sum of money to invest in a club of Reading's history and pedigree but it takes that massive sum of money to stay in the big game.

So, with Reading still in Division One but now managerless after Quinn and Gooding's departure, work began on transforming the wasteland of Smallmead.

Behind the fence the building of the hotel begins.

At the same time the construction of the final stages of the Relief Road was underway and the air all around was heavy with brown dust. An instructive, illustrated account of the technicalities of the building process and progress was given in the souvenir edition of the programme for the opening match and the interested layman is referred to that. Suffice to say that, despite a few problems caused by record rainfall (haven't we heard that before?), the construction proceeded in a seemingly confident and orderly manner. Elm Park was kept ready just in case there was any unforeseen delay that the Football League would not have looked kindly on.

In January 1998 a Visitors Centre was opened on the building site, accessed by a circuitous route via Bennet Road and Island Road, and many went along to see. Personally, I would have seen it as an act of disloyalty to the living Elm Park to go and goggle at its successor. However, in April, the Supporters' Club Committee was invited to go and have a look around and so I made my first trip to the Madejski Stadium. The late afternoon sky was heavy with black scudding clouds, though the horizon was still pale and light. The landscape was all digger-torn muddy chaos, fractured with giant puddles. The stadium looked like a war victim. The atmosphere was Mad Max meets Bladerunner. The big kick-off was 4 months away. One had to presume these people knew what they were doing. Boyd Butler, the marketing manager, greeted us with hard hats and wellies and off we went.

I had tried and succeeded in not having any preconceptions. My immediate impression was that the stadium was big, too big for the crammed in club I had known. The Lower West Stand did not feel like a lower stand once you had got up past the rain-soaked first 10 rows. The Upper West was spectacular. It was difficult to compute that this was the equivalent of Row K in C stand where I often sat in the last few years. The view was grand, good, distant. I was disappointed to see how generous the leg-room was. Having spent the first half my footballing life peering from behind six-footers on the terraces I was after some payback in the second half from seeing them squashed up in their seats! As a group I think it was fair to say that we were impressed by the building. The simple act of being there brought home to me a scary, new dimension of Reading Football Club. It was not simply going to be the same but better; it was going to be different.

No climbing over these turnstiles.

The Beauty is in the Money

Professional football, they say, is all about money now. All those non-players in suits, beavering away in the Madejski Stadium, are trying raise the money to pay the players, then to pay for new and better players and to pay them too. The paradigm of late 20th century football is this: only resources (mostly in the form of money) count, resources equate to success, resources buy players, players bring success.

Not long ago, say only 12 years ago, it was a little different. Then, poorly resourced teams like Oxford, homeless Charlton, Portsmouth, Luton and Wimbledon were in the top division and Aston Villa, Middlesbrough, Leeds, Sunderland and Manchester City were not. It was possible for smaller, well-managed clubs to build a team over a few seasons, get promotion to Division One (as was) and exist on gates of 12,000 or less. Equally it was possible for major clubs with huge potential to exist for several seasons in a lower division under bad and/or autocratic management. As football became more of a business with the advent of live TV, satellite TV, return to European competition, salaries for directors, Stock Market flotations so the tolerance of football failure diminished. Once the Premiership started in 1992 it was unacceptable from a business point of view for any major club to spend even a season outside it. Football's resources (i.e. the money the clubs can get from its individual fans and corporate sponsors) were subsequently more efficiently harvested.

Unfortunately it was also more quickly spent. Whilst Taylor-driven stadia improvements were a short-term cost (paid back by the fans over the medium term in most cases) the spiralling costs of players' wages were a more serious longer-term phenomenon. Football was replacing music and film as the domain of today's stars. Within the course of the decade the top international level of players suddenly started earning a reputed £40-50,000 a week. There was a knock-on effect right down the football ladder. The Bosman ruling, which essentially outlawed transfer fees for out-of-contract players, gave the players yet more negotiating power. Overnight players' wages became the sponge that mopped all that new wealth that football was creating and threatened to take more as well. Maybe the top ten clubs found themselves better off than before but, at Reading's level, despite there being a lot more money coming in than ever before, the club could not match revenue to costs. Most fans do not blame players as individuals for seeking to get what the market would pay them but their doing so increases expectations that they will perform to a consistently high standard.

Executive Class bar.

At the same time the football authorities have placed more of an emphasis on skilled players and skilled players cost proportionately more. It is now far harder to put together, successfully, a team of cheap-and-cheerful, well-motivated scrappers to kick your way out of a division, which used to be the only option for some poor clubs. The use of 5 substitutes, stricter refereeing, more frequent suspensions and better pitches all work against the poorer club. The Bosman ruling, and the increasing inability to keep better players for a second contract, work against the smaller club too. To progress, it is clearly a good idea not to be a poorer club. Resources mean money, money means better players, better players often mean better results. Opposing clubs are no longer feared for the size of the centre-half's thighs but for the size of the Chairman's wallet!

At Reading's sub-Premiership, sub-constant Sky TV coverage level, the most important money-creating resource is the ground itself. The economic function of the stadium is to harvest as efficiently as possible the money that the club's willing supporters are prepared to spend on football. As money-harvesting machines go Elm Park, for all its character, was about as efficient as 10 blind men with 2 blunt scythes. By contrast, the Madejski Stadium is a super new machine, capable of combining the full harvests of football, rugby, conferences, banquets and hotel accommodation.

I'm sorry if this bores you, but it's important because this is what football is about now and, as a football fan, you ought to know. If you don't like figures pass on to the next section but you'll miss some vital points.

Up and running into a half million profit in the first year, the Royal Berkshire Conference Centre was using the match day corporate hospitality facilities on a near daily basis. Planning permission was obtained in January 1999 for a 155 bed luxury hotel, due to open in Spring 2000, attached to the West Stand and Conference centre. Profits were projected to be £1.5 million a year. Ground sharing with Richmond rugby was another revenue stream worth a few hundred thousand in year one. All these new revenue streams are designed to feed regular, big money into the main business of the football club. Here, too, there would be a lot more money about.

At an individual level, going to Elm Park on a typical Saturday I would have spent about £27. My equivalent spend at the Madejski is £30. But the difference in Reading's take is double, up from £12 to £25. I now eat and drink less well and pay for my parking but my club does get the benefit of the vast majority of my spending, which is fairer because they are the reason I set foot out of the house in the first place.

You're on CCTV.

From a wider perspective, let's imagine the revenue implications of both Elm Park and the Madejski Stadium being three quarters full, as was the case several times in the seasons under review. I don't have any inside information. I'm just using educated guesswork and layman's arithmetic. The Madejski Stadium would make broadly twice as much in ticket sales from ordinary (i.e. non-corporate) supporters as Elm Park, say £200,000 versus £100,000. It costs much more to open the Madejski than Elm Park for match day but this difference is probably easily covered by extra ancillary sales of programmes, refreshments and merchandise. On the corporate side, assuming again three quarters capacity paying at full rate card price, we see an even more dramatic uplift, from about £10,000 to £25,000. (A corporate clientele of around 500 can contribute over 10% of the ticket revenue. But, there again, 90% of the ticket revenue comes from the putative 17,500 ordinary fans.) Altogether the difference in revenue on such a game may be in the order of £125,000, the great proportion of which is profit. Over 10 such games the extra profit would be over a million pounds. One begins to see how a new stadium can pay, provided it, of course, is well-attended.

The typical adult admission price has risen from £9 to £12 (pre-booked). There is a general perception that football ticket prices are high. Having worked professionally on the subject for the Premier League, the Football League and the Football Task Force, I understand that most fans actually feel most prices are now reasonable (after a period of some excess). There are, we know, people who can no longer afford to go, even in the affluent Thames Valley, but they are also plenty of people for whom the purchase of a season ticket is 'not a problem'. For the first season at the Madejski a standard adult season ticket would cost a new fan £240, just over £10 per game. After paying £10 to become a Young Royal a junior season ticket was on offer for £80, effectively a cost of £4 per game. And there were instalment plans available. Compare this supporter contribution with the cost of paying a player on a £100,000 salary (and we have a few). On the standard daily rate calculation, that fan's £240 covers the cost of employing that one player for just one morning, maybe a Tuesday morning in June, maybe one of the players who was injured all season. To cover his wages for the rest of the year would take another 219 new fans buying season tickets. It sounds a terribly large amount when you think of some of the players we've seen. But it can make financial sense.

Take Bobby Mikhailov, the Bulgarian international goalkeeper, we signed in 1995. His two year stay cannot have cost the club less than £500,000 in fees and wages. In theory he could have played 100 games, £5,000 a game at that rate.

Shiny plastic set aside for VIPs.

His international class could have saved us 10 League points a season and we could have finished higher in the League, with more ladder money and bigger gates. Those 10 points might have got us to the play-offs, which could have been worth £200,000. He could have paid for himself and more and still gone home on a free. As it was, he played only 28 games in which he was as much a liability as an asset. Lose some, win some. His predecessor, an ex-student called Shaka Hislop, did play 100 games in 2 seasons and was worth 10 points a season, a major foundation of Reading's success. Cost nothing, went for £1.6 million. How can you budget for these outcomes? You can't. You've got to trust the manager, spend and see.

Having a large season-ticket-holder base helps. Mass season-ticket-holding is one of the phenomena of 'new football'. Only 10 years ago there were just 5 clubs selling more than 10,000 season tickets (including Manchester United on 10,500). Reading had 931 then. Now you can't get into many top grounds as a home fan without one. In the last year at Elm Park, Reading sold a record 2,200. In the first year at the Madejski there were 3,800.

Season tickets are great for the club because all the money's in before the season starts and it can live on credit from the fans even if they don't turn up for the games. It cuts out the cost of handling the cash, bagging it up and taking it to the bank, and avoids the possibility of turnstile operator fraud. The electronic season tickets available towards the end of the 1998/99 season are even better because they don't require turnstile operators to view them or office staff to send out renewals. It can all be done electronically and, in theory, with great increases in efficiency.

But, for the fan, rationally what is the point of getting a season ticket for a Division Two ground that's going to hold 24,000? You'll always get in. Unless you go to every game you won't save money. You won't feel you have to go when you know it's going to be a terrible game. But, in today's game, there are other factors to consider. Season ticket holders get privileges for away games. This doesn't matter when there are only a few hundred of them but it swamps the allocations for many grounds when there are thousands. Also, a season-ticket is more convenient. You don't have to book over the phone or go all the way down to the stadium. You don't forget to go in advance and find you have to pay an extra £2 on the day. You can't pay in cash at the turnstile. You're better off with a Smart Card season ticket that automatically opens the unmanned turnstile for you and allows you to add cup-tie credit to its magic strip (not literally!) over the phone. You might as well get one, then. Goodbye, handful of metal coins. Hello, wallet containing shiny plastic!

The opening day balloons soar into the Berkshire sky.

Perfect Day

At the end of the day, as any football bore will tell you, it's what happens out there on that green rectangle that counts. The results are the gears of the operation: five good ones and you're flying in overdrive, five bad ones and you're bumping along in second.

Just 6 days after Gilkes' testimonial match the Royals' Division Two season kicked off. The first game against Wrexham was scheduled to be at home, but both sides were happy to switch to the Racecourse Ground as the Madejski Stadium neared completion. New players had been bought but two, Graeme Murty and John Polston, were already injured. Mark Reilly, the Liberian international Mass Sarr and two freshly signed Dutchman, Peter Van der Kwaak and Elroy Kromheer were added to the squad that travelled to North Wales.

Reading fans did not really know what to expect. Only three of the starting line up had been at the club more than a year and three were making their debuts. In the event the Royals were soundly beaten 3-0 and Lambert and Davies never played again. A late equaliser by Asaba got Reading a draw at Peterborough in the First Round of the League Cup in midweek. Bristol Rovers away was next and, despite taking the lead, a disjointed performance led to a 1-4 defeat. Bowen was never to play again and Tommy Burns read the riot act over players' general discipline and attitude.

But back in Reading the enthusiasm to see the new stadium was building tremendously. The optimism was unquashed by the first 2 results. There had not been such a palpable football buzz in town since the play-offs 3 years before. There was talk even of the game being a complete sell-out which would surely have been a record for a team at this level on a run of 17 defeats in 19 games!

As the deadline approached Birse, the contractors, and the Club were relaxed and confident that all would be ready for the Safety Certificate inspectors, as, indeed it all was. Elsewhere, massive traffic gridlock problems in South Reading were envisaged as 20,000 people converged on an unfamiliar stadium with only one vehicle traffic access point.

The Supporters' Club felt the need to mark some connection or bond of continuity between Elm Park and the Madejski Stadium as nothing physical had been brought across.

The parachutist lands.

A pint inside the ground for the first time.

The new Mass – iah.

So, as a symbolic gesture, we arranged to bring some grass cuttings from the Elm Park pitch and scatter them in the goalmouths of the Madejski Stadium as part of the opening day programme. The day before the big day I went into Elm Park to pick up the cuttings. It was a lovely, still, summer's afternoon. I stood on the centre spot, no one shouting at me now, to look around. The South Bank clock had stopped at the very unfootball time of 1.17. Somebody, as a mark of respect, should have turned the hands to quarter to five. (Instead, somebody was very soon to nick the hands before the clock could be auctioned!) It really did feel that Elm Park was now gone and I was excited about going to the new place tomorrow.

The following day about 60 fans marched from the gates of the South Bank to the Madejski Stadium bearing the grass cuttings. We went by the most direct route possible missing any major roads, south through Prospect Park, down into the Southcote estate and on to the stony track leading out to the badlands beyond. Once under the rail bridges, with the desolate rattle of freight trains overhead, we picked up the towpath of the Kennet&Avon canal, walked past the gaily coloured barges and their surprised owners, over the Holybrook and down to the brick-red buildings of Fobney Lock. Turning left here away from the canal, we had left the clutches of West Reading and were now poised at the end of a dirt track to met South Reading. As the view opened out the Island Road rubbish dump was to our right, but straight ahead, and still a mile away on the horizon, was the gleaming whiteness of the Madejski Stadium, a celestial city amid a scrubby wasteland, as a prophet might have said. "Is that it, then?" someone grunted.

Shortly, having battled past the traffic snake, we were there – much earlier than we needed to be. But already the aprons outside the turnstiles were busy with hooped figures and the atmosphere was cup-tie. There was nothing to do and nowhere to go except the newly opened club shop, the Megastore. That day it doubled the record takings for the club shop.

The sun was out as we passed through the turnstiles. It was nothing like my previous visit. It was clean, white and big. We went into the Upper West Stand concourses where there were literally people touching and stroking the walls and bars, saying *"This can't be Reading!"* There was delight on most faces and shock on a few. The man I waited to come from Japan all those years ago in the Foresters and I, now with our families, took our seats. By pure coincidence, the man already sat on my right happened to be my partner when we won the West Reading Schools Wheelbarrow Race in 1966. Straightaway, we saw the bonds of the old community could exist here also! The brass band played, the stars of yesteryear waved to the crowd, the skydivers dived, the balloons soared, the grass-scatterers scattered and Stuart Hall harrumphed around on the pitch and over the loudspeaker and the stadium steadily filled with blue-and-white hooped shirts.

A lavish stage.

Those who walked down Acre Road reported seeing the stadium aloft on its mound looking like a mini-Wembley and their progress was slowed by a narrow set of steps up the slope. The kick-off was delayed 15 minutes and people again shuffled around the queues at the concourse bars that had been opened.

And then, to the sound of the theme of 2001- A Space Odyssey, the crowd gathered, waited and finally, as the players emerged from the tunnel, simply roared. Just a huge wordless roar that suggested the waiting was at last over. The new era had begun.

The Royals, with a makeshift back four in front of the uncertain van der Kwaak, were as nervous as kittens but high on adrenalin. Luton lost one player, injured after 10 minutes, and another 7 minutes later. In between, the Reading won a corner on the right. Caskey took it, Kromheer met it with a downward header which was blocked by Mass Sarr. The ball ran to Grant Brebner, just beyond the penalty spot, who thrashed it right-footed into the back of the South Stand net and raced away in celebration. From that moment on it was Reading's day. Both attacks were in the ascendant, Luton looking the more organised and having the better chances but frustrated by van der Kwaak and the woodwork. At the other end, Mass Sarr, on his home debut, turned in a virtuoso performance that completely won over the packed East Stand, desperate for a new hero. Somehow he could not quite get the goal he deserved but he helped make the second. Houghton picked the ball up on the edge of his own penalty area, played a one-two with McIntyre then floated the return out to the left. Sarr, coming in-field to meet it, took it on his left thigh, leaving his marker for dead, then gently played it inside for McIntyre to drill home from 15 yards. It was a goal of skill, grace and invention, one perhaps that spoke of great things to come. Sadly, McIntyre tore his hamstring shortly after and Sarr went off holding his too. A clinching third goal from Robert Fleck came five minutes from the end from another excellent piece of football and the crowd was ready to go home very happy.

Us walkers, trespassing our way back up the unfinished dual carriageway and then along the canal, were fine and back to West Reading within the hour. Those who relied on cars were stuck in the car park, and those who relied on buses faced severe delays that took the edge off the day. Residents in the Whitley area, now faced with what the residents of West Reading had borne more or less stoically for years, complained that the traffic and parking had made them 'prisoners in their homes'. That apart, the whole day was generally judged a great success.

Whilst the initial verdict on the stadium was very clear it seemed the number of people who attended the match would never be so. 3 turnstile counters had stuck on implausibly low numbers so the official attendance figure was given as 18,108. The club had said during the week over 20,000 tickets were sold and felt the real figure in the ground was nearer to 22,000.

Afterwards, there were plaudits aplenty for the design of the stadium: *"the first sight of the interior of the playing bowl literally takes the breath away"* (Reading Chronicle), *"the stadium has a clarity of vision and handsomeness of space and civility that very few in the Premiership can better"* (The Times), *"the design is strong and clean, it's blue-and-white wraparound stands drop sharply to the touchlines and vision is unobstructed"* (Daily Telegraph), *"lavish stage"* (Sunday Mirror) and, somewhat hurtfully, *"out of place at this level"* (The Guardian). The unfolding season would hopefully render The Guardian's judgement temporary.

Concourse life

Later in the year Kingsley joins the drama, from an offside position.

'The design is strong and clean'.

'Straight lines and clarity'.

The old groundsman surveys the new ground.

New Vision Versus Old Reality

For the first couple of weeks, fans were absorbed and overwhelmed by how good the Madejski Stadium was as a place to watch football. Sure, there were a lot of low level gripes about queues, parking and the like, but most people were happy to give the club the benefit of the doubt that these 'teething troubles' would be overcome. The fans' general response was very favourable. There had been a lot of talk from the club about how good the stadium would be. The surprise was that it had been delivered. Forgive us, but being Reading fans for many years has bred a certain cynicism.

The view was excellent and uninterrupted, the seats were comfortable and spacious, the toilets were clean and capacious and the refreshments were available if a little expensive. Those match-goers who value toilet and refreshment facilities as much as football itself could never cite the lack of them as an excuse not to come again. This was all great and gratefully received. But, as many long-standing fans soon realised, it seemed part of a wider, and unpublicised, vision that they found a little unsettling. There was a sense of total revolution and of the stadium taking over the football club. Almost everything had to be new.

It started with the signage on the roads – all the signs were to the Madejski Stadium, not to Reading FC. The telephones were answered 'Madejski Stadium' not 'Reading Football Club', the tickets were Madejski Stadium tickets and there was no sign on the outside or the inside of the stadium to say this was the home of Reading Football Club. Instead we seemed to have equal status with Richmond Rugby Football Club.

It had been known since May that we would be ground-sharing with Richmond, a club formerly based in the south west of London, a large city some 40 miles downstream of the Thames from Reading. Richmond were part of the new vision too, signing a three year agreement to share all facilities, shops and bars too, at the Madejski Stadium. It had not been appreciated how much of a stake Richmond were to have in the identity of the stadium. They were happy to describe themselves, incorrectly, as co-tenants of the stadium to the national media and their presence and sensibilities essentially blocked Reading's branding of the stadium as their own. For instance, all but one of the concourse bars were given bland names that could apply to either sport. We liked the new stadium. We wanted to shout to the world, it's ours!

Richmond had an aggressive high-risk strategy of attempting to establish, very quickly, a first class rugby club in the Thames

Alien life form descending.

Valley whilst continuing to hold on to and bus down their existing fan base. They promoted themselves extensively in the local community and schools, giving away thousands of free tickets. Three times they had crowds of around 10,000 but for the most part they played in front of half that number or less. Reading remained very much a football town. In March 1999, Richmond's major investor withdrew support and soon after they folded up. Reading made several hundred thousand pounds from the arrangement but had to bear a great deal of criticism about the poor state of the pitch.

Ground-sharing inevitably lessens the intimacy between the fan and the ground. You can see all your team's matches but still not be sure of seeing everything of sporting significance that happens in the ground. Something else is going on in *your* place while you're not there. That feeling of exclusivity is likely, though, to be a luxury of the old days. There is not much financial sense in putting up a £25 million stadium and only using it 25 times a year when it could be used 40 or more times. Groundsharing, in some form, will probably come again.

So the Richmond RFC badge, along with that of Reading Football Club and the Royal Berkshire Conference Centre, appeared all over, almost as a sub-brand of the main entity, the stadium itself. There was, I felt, a desperate desire from the club management to get away from cramped, old Elm Park, and all that it stood for, as fast as it possibly could. In 'image' terms there were two ways of handling the transition. One could emphasise the continuity of the life of the club from one place to another or one could go for as near complete a break as possible. Whether by desire or accident or a combination of both, the club took the latter route.

In Tommy Burns, a manager of new style and stature had already been appointed. Within the space of his first ten games he had brought in a dozen new young, clean-cut players, mostly from outside the Football League, and effectively said goodbye to a dozen more, including a few 'long-standing servants' like Lovell, Morley, Wdowczyk and Lambert.

The kit changed somewhat. Whilst retaining the blue-and-white hooped shirts, blue shorts replaced the traditional white. This, combined with the odd 'bleeding' or 'seeping' effect of the blue into the white hoops, gave the players a heavier look and made them appear a little weighed down.

The badge changed as we all knew it would. The much-loved Elms design had been revived for a final season to replace Ian Branfoot's unimaginative striped shield.

Tommy Burns, man with a mission.

This IS Reading Football Club.

A clean and controlled environment.

In the meantime the fans had chorused down a number of designs based on a lion and the word 'Royals'. The club's brief then asked for a dynamic, forward-looking design for the new era. In due course, a neat circular design using the convention of heraldic quarters, featuring both a crown and a lion on a red background and centred on a brown leather football, appeared on merchandise and literature everywhere.

The volume on the nickname 'Royals' was turned up. It's a name that does not sit easily because it does not express a fundamental truth about the club or the town. Clearly Reading is not a Royal place with a palace (unlike Windsor&Eton FC – 'the Royalists') but nor is 'the Royals' an obvious, ironic mickey-take like Slough Town's 'the Rebels'. 'The Royals' was selected as a successor to 'the Biscuitmen' - something that I never heard anyone use in normal conversation! - by manager Charlie Hurley when Huntley&Palmers shut down in 1976. Its basis is a reference to Royal Berkshire. It makes a good chant, "Come on, You Royaaaaals", but it is hard to take it credibly much further. Fans call their team 'Reading'. However, the local media had always loved the new nickname and so increasingly did the club.

So, on top of the breathtaking difference of the view of the pitch, in a new stadium in a new part of town, came the Royals in their new kit and badge, with plenty of unknown faces in the team. Whilst getting to the stadium could still feel like an away trip, it was understandable that fans cried out for a sign, a literal sign outside, to say they were at home. And, after a while, a sign saying 'Reading FC' appeared over the players tunnel and, eventually (after planning permission had been obtained) in the New Year, the new badge in giant-size was affixed in two places to the outside walls. No parallel option was offered to Richmond and honour was satisfied.

There were calls for links with the past from fans. One wrote, "I think it would be appropriate if the East Stand were named after Robin Friday" to which the programme replied, "as far as the stand names go, they will be named after companies who sponsor the club. It is their contribution that makes the club successful and is common practice in football". Another asked if there were any plans to bring items over from Elm Park. "There is very little that can be brought from Elm Park" (in fact nothing was) "…if you feel that moving to Madejski means that history is not respected you are wrong. The bars in the East Stand will refer to the history of the club. The programme has all the club history in various features. The Supporters' Club will keep the Elm Park spirit alive and last but not least we all have memories."

The reply went on to state that Reading FC was a 'brand' and that the brand in commercial terms was very important.

But it was less emphatic about what the characteristics of this brand had formerly been or whether these elements were still deemed to be desirable. The embracing of 'new football' went on in other areas too. The share capital of the club was still a ridiculously low £50,000 so John Madejski initiated a rights issue which had the effect of capitalising many of the loans he had made to the club, thus putting his involvement in the business on a more permanent basis.

Unobstructed views.

It was also likely to have increased his stake to around the 90% mark. Director of Youth Football, John Stephenson, embarked on a campaign to bring FA Academy Status to Reading. The youth policy had been through one of its periodic phases of neglect with no players coming through to established first-team status for some years. As part of the serious overall long-term investment in the club, big efforts would be made to revolutionise the approach to youth development.

New vision.

Parky pelts over to his people.

In February 1999 the application was successful and Reading became only the 36th Academy status club in the country. Soon after, Stephenson reported, "We have recruited a Science Officer to coordinate the delivery of the science programme to our academy". It doesn't sound as though those lads will spend too much time sweeping the terraces!

And finally, on the pitch, the first team was due for modernisation. Tommy Burns came with a reputation as a good footballing manager, highly thought of in influential circles. One was never quite sure what Terry Bullivant's philosophy was but Burns was a man for getting it down, passing it around neatly, patiently if necessary, and waiting for the openings to come. He started with a 4-5-1 formation in the belief that the wide players would quickly supplement the attack. Long ball was out, long ball would not help the club progress when we got back to Division One. Several players with fashionable Continental or Premiership reserve backgrounds were recruited.

The unstated new vision seemed to be about neat, clever football outwitting the division in front of large crowds of highly satisfied new fans spending 4 or 5 hours and £40 or £50 at the stadium. One club official talked to me about promoting "a clean, controlled environment that might take some supporters a little while to get used to". One player wrote "we don't expect it to be a walk-over" which was fair enough, but the fact he thought he needed to say that is telling in itself. Reading had spent 52 out of 71 League seasons at this level and won promotion from it just three times. Some rivals in the division saw a touch of arrogance about Reading now and the disastrous early results suggested some unreality in the aspirations. Burns's tactics needed confident players but his early selections were full of changes and players were empty of self-belief. In adversity, some went into their shells. One fan said, "I didn't think it could get any worse after last season but I was wrong". Within five games the Royals were employing a 'more pragmatic' tactical approach. Within 10 games, Phil Parkinson, briefly threatened with exile by transfer to Wycombe, was back in midfield with the captain's armband on. Parky was a man the fans knew and trusted, a man who typified the spirit that was in the club a few years ago. Parky belonged to the past as well as the present. Parky helped bridge the transition to the new ground.

He pelted out of the tunnel first, arms pumping, straight over to the fans in the East Stand. On his own. With him back in the number 4 shirt (and with other changes too) the season began to turn round. He was to win Player of the Year, again. As the new vision and the old reality soon merged into the new reality he was the fans' presence on the pitch.

Euch! Aargh! Crumbs! Och!

The Groundhog Game

Four days after the Luton match, a crowd of over 9,000 came to watch the Royals under the Madejski Stadium lights for the first time. For a First Round League Cup tie this was an exceptionally good gate but even so, other than in the East Stand where it appeared more than half the crowd were gathered, the atmosphere was rather missing. Ticketing and turnstile problems led to another delayed kick-off and angry customers outside, but inside the ground all was well. The floodlights were arranged along the side of the roofs of the East and West Stands, rather than on pylons, and were so brilliantly bright that the spectator almost lost the sense of the night sky beyond. One photographer claimed they were the best he had ever worked under. Reading created lots of early chances but beat Peterborough less comfortably than 2-0 might suggest. In a way this was the precursor of the 'Groundhog game'.

In the film "Groundhog Day" every day is the same. After a while, matches at the Madejski Stadium took on a remarkably similar aspect. There would be a crowd of 8,000 to 10,000. Reading would kick to the South Stand. The opposition would spend the first few minutes in a panic as they adjusted their minds to Reading's new status and surroundings. Reading would have most of the play in the first half and score but fail to kill the game off. In the second half the Royals would then begin to back pedal and look nervous, rely on their woodwork and finally give away a late goal for a 1-1 draw. The 2nd, 3rd, 6th and 11th League games at the Madejski followed this pattern exactly, while the 8th varied by ending 3-3 and the 5th 0-0. In the 7th Reading did not concede a late equaliser while in the 4th, having conceded the equaliser Reading went on to win 2-1. I suppose it helped people settle down, but it also quickly added frustrations about the team to those that fans were having about the operation of the stadium. In short, the honeymoon did not last long.

In fact, the Royals were jeered off after only the second League game! Burnley were the visitors and an obviously poor side. Williams tapped Reading into an early lead and was promptly kicked up in the air by Peter Swan who thus claimed the distinction of being the first man sent off at the Madejski Stadium. Dispirited and down to 10 men the Clarets should have been crushed. But with half an hour to go they found themselves still in the game and began to push forward. It was no surprise when Andy Payton drifted past two defenders to slide home an equaliser 15 minutes from time. It was vital for the Royals to score the winner, but Caskey's effort that hit the bar in the last minute added to, rather than assuaged, the frustration of the fans.

"I'll be back on Venus before you're out of that car park".

Afterwards, the police thought it would be a good idea to declare Acre Road 'a sterile area' and not let any vehicles down it. This meant one exit point, the single-file, narrow winding track round the back to Bennet Road. Thousands, including young kids with school the next day, were still stuck in the car park an hour or more after the game, dwelling on that late equaliser.

More bad away results followed before the visit of newly promoted Colchester. Panicking at the start, a flick of brilliance from Mass Sarr opened them up for the first goal. But the second wouldn't come and well before half-time the Royals were in nervous retreat again, a team with no confidence even 1-0 up on a ground they had never been behind on. Colchester sensed this and laid siege in the second half. The bar and posts were as overworked as our defence and, finally, a minute from the end they bundled in an equaliser from a corner that should have been cleared. Arrgh. Perhaps the weight of expectation from the new stadium, on top of a long run of bad form, was getting to the team. The Royals then went out of the League Cup 1-4 on aggregate to Barnsley, Caskey's last minute penalty in the 1-1 home leg preserving the unbeaten ground record. The slide must stop somewhere and struggling Macclesfield, in only their second League season, looked as good a place as any. The Royals lost 1-2 and Booty and Reilly were never to play again. This was the Royals 15th successive away defeat in the League and it left them in the bottom four of a division many had hoped they could win.

Then, as sometimes happens, things suddenly changed for the better. After a great opening goal from the on-form Martin Williams, Reading surprisingly won 2-0 at promotion-challenging Walsall. For the visit of League-leaders Stoke, more than 13,000 came to see the Reading revival continue. Stoke missed early chances and Reading combined for a goal of rare quality to gain their customary half-time lead. The large and vociferous Stoke following were distraught at not being able to buy pints at half-time so started attacking the bar areas in the first outbreak of trouble the new ground had seen. In the second half the Royals gave away the customary daft goal by not marking at the far post. This time the team were so angered they roused themselves to score a deserved winner to huge acclaim. Though we had given the rest of the division an 8 game start the season looked back on track.

Sadly it was back to Groundhog time with a 0-0 draw against a spoiling Gillingham on a windy afternoon with a pitch cut long for rugby, and 4 days later another 1-1 against Blackpool. For 85 minutes the unambitious Seasiders held out and the players were obviously as frustrated as the fans as our patient football got nowhere. Then Williams spun and lashed the ball, almost in anger, into the top corner for what surely was the winner.

Macca lets off steam.

Parky, choked.

Come on, URZ.

Suddenly, and for no seemingly good reason, new signing Chris Casper was sent off and before the Royals could reorganise Blackpool equalised with a long shot off the post. More points lost, more traffic to sit and fume in.

Yet more away wins followed. You wait 8 months for one then get four in a row! York were next up at home and everything happened to custom, with the crowd now dreading the late equaliser. This time it never came and Reading had a third home win to go with four draws. The opposition had yet to score a League goal at the North Stand end though most, York included, seemed to have hit the woodwork. A victory on Saturday over the challenging Bournemouth would set the season up nicely.

Wolves may have been our most engaging modern day opponents and the kind of club the Royals would like to pitch themselves against regularly. They represented the good, new days. Bournemouth, for me, represented the other part of Reading's existence, the routine, workaday struggle to get out of the bottom two divisions. The failure to do so was usually indicated by the presence of Bournemouth on the fixture card: 32 seasons in a row up to 1970, 45 times in all, more League visits to Elm Park than any other club and many hard, low-scoring games in recent years. The Cherries had managed just three years (compared with our eleven) out of the lower divisions but the desire to escape was as strong as ever.

Another 13,000 crowd on a sunny afternoon, another decent, competitive atmosphere and a game well worth winning. Exactly what the stadium was built for. Caskey scored a good goal from Sarr's pass, then Bournemouth penetrated our North Stand goal for the first time. In another great move, Williams gave Reading a half-time lead. A blatant dive led to a second Bournemouth equaliser from the penalty spot then, near the end, skipper Phil Parkinson rose to meet a corner and powered a header in off the post. Storybook stuff to kick-start the season and get the confidence flowing right around the club. No doubt that this was the stadium's best game so far. And then, in injury time, a long ball was allowed to bounce into the penalty area and a fortunate foot swept it past Scott Howie for 3-3. Was there no end to this? 5 times in 7 games the opposition had scored a late equaliser. "Choked," said Parky afterwards. "We could have been on a real high."

A win would have put the Royals eighth in the table only six weeks after languishing in 21st position. As it was, Reading had still won 5 and drawn 3 of the last 8 games, and Tommy Burns was visited with the curse of the 'Manager of the Month' award for October. The disappointment of the Bournemouth game had taken its toll and four days later the unbeaten record of 'Fortress Madejski' was gone.

Lion in wait.

Wigan were the third of four visitors in the space of 10 days as the fixture list worked overtime getting fans used to their new surroundings. They scored early from a dubious penalty, defended stoutly and strangled the game to run out unmemorable 1-0 winners. It was all a bit too 'lower division' for most of Reading's new look team. Some said it was a mixed blessing to lose the unbeaten home record as the fact of it was weighing on the players' minds. Others felt that some of the magical newness of the Madejski Stadium had gone. It was mortal now. Reading could lose here too!

And lose again we did, three days later as Stoke City returned for a FA Cup First Round tie. There were 3,000 fewer people in the crowd than for the League match and the whole atmosphere felt lower key. Such is the response of the modern fan to the world's oldest and once most exciting competition. Stoke scored from a break in the first half, Reading were denied a good penalty shout in the second and were then out of the Cup. Just the League to concentrate on now, with 29 games to go. What a contrast with last season's 12 cup matches. Sky TV had brought their cameras to cover this match in an unusual 'extended highlights' format screened early that evening. This was the first and only TV football coverage from the Madejski Stadium in its debut season.

So, in spite of the heavy influence of the Groundhog game, the new ground had, by now, seen most of what life in football routinely offers: wins, draws, defeats, goals at either end, goals and no goals, penalties and sendings-off for both sides, a spot of trouble in the crowd, joy, excitement, frustration, anger, big crowds and smaller crowds. Everything but rain and a really great game.

It does not generally take people long to adapt to new circumstances however radical and however long they had lived in the old ways. By November, Reading fans were getting used to the Madejski Stadium. But before examining how the faithful (and the newly converted) were taking to a football cultural revolution, let us take a final look down the Tilehurst Road to record what happened to the buildings of Elm Park.

Rusting Tin & Shiny Plastic

The Demolition of Elm Park

After the testimonials and the veteran fans' tournament were over, Elm Park first came under the auctioneer's hammer and then the demolisher's bulldozer. Thimbleby&Shorland, sounding, and indeed looking, splendidly Dickensian, put a great deal of work into this most curious of auctions. A catalogue was produced and it spanned precious football relics like the 19th century turnstiles and mundane artefacts of modern corporate entertainment like the ice-making machines.

On a very wet Sunday lunchtime, September 27th, 200 or so bidders and onlookers gathered, mostly a mix of loyal collector-fans and scavengers from non-League football clubs. There were many satisfied buyers at keen prices. The floodlight pylons went unsold though their bulbs found another life elsewhere. Less than a penalty area's worth of turf was sold and thereafter it was 'help yourself'.

A few days later the Supporters' Club Committee went in to empty the South Bank of its 'just possibly saleable' programme stock. We formed a chain-gang working by candlelight and from time to time saw figures flitting on the other side pitch picking up their auction purchases or just nosing. Each of us took time to break away and spend a minute in personal reflection. I stood in my old place in the middle of the South Bank not really knowing what to think. I was 'goodbyed out'!

For a few days, Elm Park settled in unsupervised silence, a danger to the local trespassing youth and a fire hazard to inhabitants of Norfolk Road. Then, in mid-October, the first bulldozer came through behind the directors' car park and just ate its way into the Town End, just chewed a hole right through. For some reason I had imagined it would be much more difficult to demolish bare, concrete terracing.

That sortie was just to establish demolishers' 'rights' to the site. The first task was to pull down the wooden, fire-risky 1926 stand. Bit by bit it was emptied and cleared. A few old notices and programmes were found but no secret trophy suggesting that Reading had superseded West Auckland as world champions in 1915 in a match long forgotten about! Then the structure of the stand was pulled forward on to the pitch and carted away. Norfolk Road could now, for a year or so, see the Tilehurst Road. The pitch itself was quickly, and wilfully it seemed, churned up. The barriers were burnt off with welding torches. The diggers ate away at both ends from the Norfolk Road side before starting on the massive concrete meal of the South Bank. Much of the rubble and concrete was loaded into the lorries of John Mould and presumably taken to his stone-crushing plant down at, ironically, Smallmead. Ghoulishly, half not wanting to go, I was drawn along to watch whenever I was in Reading. I was never alone there though. One Sunday afternoon, in half an hour, I counted 20 people, some wearing scarves and most with cameras, mournfully wandering about.

"Pitch is cutting up a bit early this season".

Finally, one foggy November night, having just exchanged contracts to sell my late parents' home, my home too for many years, I walked to the car park by the Rendezvous to say a complementary farewell to the old ground. But, eerily, I could see nothing of Elm Park, just yards away surely through the grey gloom, except perhaps a twisted girder pointing south.

You'll never take the South Bank.

Doom.

An old friend fades away.

Reading Versus Bristol Rovers ; trauma in the making.

Christmas and League Trauma

Up until the end of the year, the Royals made steady progress. Northampton were outclassed 1-0 in their own new stadium and then Reading came from behind to beat struggling Lincoln 2-1. Mass Sarr scored his first goal, a brilliant winner, streaking down the left wing to shoot home but the Liberian wasn't bedding in well. The sending off at Preston had rattled him and then came a family tragedy. The skill was obviously there but he had not settled to the tempo and the all-out effort of Division 2 and he was becoming a peripheral figure. Youngster Byron Glasgow had fought his way into a long run in the side, joining Parkinson, Primus, Caskey, Williams and, briefly, Roach from last season's side. Chris Casper, signed from Manchester United, had become a key figure in the centre of a back five while keeper Howie was beginning to look more assured.

Sarr scored again in a fortunate 1-1 at Millwall but was soon to disappear from the starting 11. The Groundhog game reappeared at the Madejski with Oldham taking a most undeserved point in another 1-1. The refrain, "We should have had the game won by half-time" was heard then and at the next game when Notts. County were beaten 1-0 in front of a large holiday crowd. Nobody could get a second goal and, though the Royals were now ninth with games in hand, there was a feeling the team was skating on thin ice whilst still not generating much excitement.

Thus defeat in the first game of the New Year was not surprising. Chesterfield were dogged and well-organised. With a gift of two first-half goals they had enough left for victory as Reading finally poured forward through the rain. Sarr cracked one goal but, despite throwing the giant Kromheer up and launching long balls at him, a second did not follow. Booed off again. The next week brought another home game, the fourth in a spell of five consecutive home matches. In all we would play 10 times at home in 11 weeks and only twice away. This was total immersion therapy in the Madejski experience! We beat Wrexham 4-0, helped by some crisp play, two soft penalties and an opposition that actually laid down and died for a change. Perhaps a good, solid win that showed our potential difference in class was just the result to get the players to relax and enjoy playing in the stadium.

The season was just past the half way mark and the top two clubs, Fulham and Walsall, were realistically out of our sights. But Gillingham, in the play-off positions, were only 4 points ahead and we had a game in hand. Sneaking up on the rails? In the midweek Burns bought Andy Gurney from Torquay and the local media were getting a little excited about the visit of Bristol Rovers.

It's new, it's cute, it's footie.

Though they had trounced Reading 4-1 early on, they were in the bottom half of the division and a club we would usually beat.

The pitch was very clearly losing a lot of grass as Richmond's activities became more frequent. The Royals were without Brebner and Casper while new man Gurney took Sarr's place. Rovers brought a large and noisy support in a crowd of over 13,000. Once again, Reading just did not get started. Time and again Rovers played their wide men into the by-line and only thanks to some atrocious finishing and excellent goalkeeping was the half-time score 0-0. No changes were made at half-time and, it is true, Rovers did not get to the by-line as much in the second half. Instead they pretty much ran through the middle and scored at will. "A horrendous catalogue" Burns called it afterwards and every goal was some kind of howler. The fourth was virtually walked in past half a dozen hooped shirts. Usually some form of dignity-saving self-preservation kicks in to prevent a total rout but, with the home crowd literally leaving in their thousands, two more were given away in the last two minutes to the awful glee of the Rovers following. My mate who left at 0-4 said, "There's going to be history made here today and I don't want to see it." And it was too, 0-6, Reading's worst-ever home League defeat in only the stadium's 15th game. Worse than any experienced in more than 1,500 League games at Elm Park. Something to get away from as fast as you can, only you can't because you're trapped by the traffic in the car park, listening to the rest of the goals going in. Arrgh. End of promotion chances? Hell, it felt like it. Deep down you know you cannot have a performance like that and go up because it traumatises the side. But three points for a win and play-offs can lead to funny outcomes.

Glad to get away from home at last, the Royals took the Groundhog game on tour for a couple more 1-1s. See how the rest of the country likes it! When Reading next played at the Madejski one of the big questions would be the size of the crowd. How many, like my mate, would have called it a day for the season? Surprisingly very few. Nearly 9,500 came and not many from Walsall, in comparison with the hordes from Bristol. The Royals again were flat from the start. On loan striker Tony Thorpe made little impression and Williams was badly injured. He went off, for the rest of the season, on a motorised stretcher wagon which, according to the Evening Post, "was greeted with a mixture of laughter and derision". Apparently the stretcher was on loan too for a trial period and, for some disillusioned fans, it emphasised the gulf between the showiness of the presentation and the shoddiness of the play. Walsall won 1-0. Thorpe later went back to wherever but the stretcher stayed on to become 'a character' (ner ner, ner ner!), even if purists still find the sight of tyre tracks on the field of play offensive.

The following week at Turf Moor, Burnley took part in Groundhog II, refining their contribution this time to an injury time equaliser, having been wiped all over the floor by a much more lively Reading. The season was in danger of disintegrating but there was yet one more upward bound to come on this roller-coaster year.

Mass Sarr dug in, in the dug out.

Manager Burns in pressure cooker.

We're getting there.

"How's it going in your new stadium ?"

Throughout the season, fans of other clubs asked me "How was it going in the new stadium?" The Madejski Stadium had received national acclaim as a building, while the 6.06 radio phone-in football programme had publicised its traffic difficulties. There was also the surprise that Reading should build a stadium far bigger than its generally accepted crowd potential. In short, this was not the Reading the rest of football knew either.

After six months and 17 games the answer 'It's early days yet' would no longer fit (though of course it was still true). The Elm Park regulars were getting used to match-going 21st century style, while a new group of fans who knew little of the past had joined in. Many of the practical teething troubles were sorted. The club had made a big effort to listen and respond to complaints made in letters, the media and the Fans Forum. By 19th December, the fanzine, The Whiff, sardonically commented, "Decent loos, edible food served in covered areas, proper facilities for the disabled, women and families, these things are good, they are welcome but seem strange to those of us who cut our football teeth on the South Bank... it would be nice to have a moan but things are going okay at the moment."

One great fear had been that the notorious Whitley Whiff, a smell that had emanated from the surrounding sewage works since 1926, would be a regular part of the Madejski match day experience, hence the title of the fanzine. But land reclamation work and anti-pollution measures on the nearby streams had a great effect in removing the smell. So to say the new place doesn't smell like a toilet was actually a major plus point!

The car park charge quickly came down from £5 to £3. The puddled potholes were filled in and lights put up so getting back to your car was no longer a walk across the Somme at midnight. Bits of new road opened from time to time, to one's sudden surprise, and the speedway car park became a backwater rather than a main thoroughfare. Other sections opened for pedestrian traffic only, and strolling down empty, rubble strewn dual carriageways added to the sense of unreality. We will forget all this within months when the traffic is roaring, or nose-to-tail, up the A33 just as we have forgotten the time in 1986 when the entire length of the Tilehurst Road was dug up and traffic-free.

It took twice as long to walk to the Madejski Stadium from the town centre as it did to Elm Park, 50 minutes as opposed to 25 and a challenge that not many undertook.

Betting man.

It was back to the buses as the council and the club put together a transport package to take as many cars off the road as possible. A shuttle service at 50p return was run from the town centre and special services introduced from outlying suburbs. The Rose&Thistle pub in west Reading sought to keep its football trade by introducing a 'drink and ride' bus which ran throughout the season. On a couple of occasions there were simply not enough buses or drivers to take fans home and after one dismal defeat I saw hundreds waiting stranded in the rain and dark with nowhere to go and no place to shelter.

The narrow flight of stairs that led from the East Stand down to Hurst Way and made the national press' jaws drop and whisper 'Ibrox' on the opening day was first fenced off and later removed. The ticket offices quickly needed enlarging to cope with the cash and non pre-booked custom.

There was a no smoking policy in the stadium 'bowl' from the start which meant smokers smoking furiously in the concourses at half-time and everyone gasping in the fug until a new ventilation system was brought in. The much-vaunted electronic scoreboard did not make its first appearance until November (but still beat new signings Polston and Murty!). The short-lived Elm Park scoreboard of the 1970s stuck when trying to record a goal for the first time. The scorer's name? Adrian Glue of Reading Reserves! True story - they don't make them like that any more.

All the concourse bars were opened by October, queuing systems introduced and gradually a few tip-up seats and ledges to put drinks on were installed, lessening the scramble for the privilege of resting your pint on top of a waste-bin. Above the East Stand concourse there was, for the £25 a year members, the Shooters Bar which could hold about 500 in surroundings of light wood and chrome several grades up from the Rendezvous, and enlivened by large video screens showing the latest on satellite TV. Shooters was also designed to have a use throughout the week as an 'executive' bar and bistro for when the executives arrived in the surrounding offices. Meanwhile the Supporters' Club opened a shop in the East Stand concourse and the bookies took up their stations in all stands. It was coming together.

Inside, the club had made the wise decisions to transfer the South Bank support and atmosphere to the East Stand, running along the side of the pitch as the South Bank had done, and to keep this part of the ground as unreserved seating for most games. The East Stand held 7,500 fans, about the same as the old South Bank. Unreserved seating retained some of the freedoms of terrace days; to go where you want so long as someone else isn't there first, to meet mates in the ground and be able to sit with them, to avoid people who got on your nerves, to just get a different view from game to game or during a

'Shooters Bar' midweek ; waiting for the executives.

The 'South Bank' bar on the East Stand concourse.

Sitting room only.

game itself, and to allow the singers to get together en masse. These were all things lost to the Premiership's reserved seated environments and were all elements that contributed to the East Stand's popularity during the season and sell-out status at big games. Some season ticket holders complained that they could not use their chosen seats but in a poll over 75% of fans there approved of the scheme.

The atmosphere in the stadium was different from Elm Park. First of all, away fans had a far better deal. Potentially they had twice as many tickets available. In fact, there were more places for away fans at the Madejski than in every Premiership ground but Wimbledon. And they had a roof now, dammit. Gone were the days of "You're getting wet, you're getting wet, we're not." A 1,000 or so away fans sounded louder and 3,000 or more much louder than at Elm Park. A home advantage seemed to have disappeared.

Reading fans responded for the bigger games but it seemed to need 12,000 or more and a sizeable away support to get the atmosphere going. The capacity of the stadium is 24,000 and with 12,000 in is therefore half-empty. To my eyes empty seats stick out as 'not being filled' far more than empty spaces on terraces. On average the Madejski Stadium was less than half-full while Elm Park in its last season was two thirds full. The sense of closeness and intensity was lessened. It may have been this, it may have been the football, it may have been the lack of any good, or local, derby floodlit matches or it may simply be the fact of all-seater stadia but the atmosphere wasn't quite what it was. A band was tried at the Chesterfield match and went down fairly well but it was not yet the spine-tingling stuff of old.

Some ex-South Bankers did what they could to keep the old ways alive by standing to sing. They had bought tickets together at the back to stay out of people's way but it was simply legally not on. There was a new, increased and often not locally-sourced stewarding presence which came into conflict with the 'standing' fans. Bad feelings escalated in the south-east corner of the stadium as the safety regulations were strictly enforced by the orange jacketed so-called Tango squad. Eventually meetings between fans' groups and the club resulted in a more 'softly softly' approach and a recognition by the fans of the laws of the new era. There was a laugh in it, though, during the Notts. County match. A male streaker (bottom half only, God, it was cold that day) appeared out of the North Stand and stood in the penalty area. Nothing happened so he started to prance around taking imaginary kicks. Still nothing from the stewards and the crowd began to wonder. Then, at speed, out of the West Stand came a burly Tango. The streaker waited to the last possible moment, neatly sidestepped the Tango's floundering dive and legged it up the stairs and out into the concourse to huge cheers.

Rain clears the front rows.

Just asking to be Tangoed.

Goal !

(He was caught and banned but he wasn't a Reading fan so what the hell!) It broke the ice a bit.

It rained surprisingly little during the course of the season but during the Chesterfield match it came down in buckets and one design 'issue' was confirmed. The front ten or so rows, depending on the wind direction, got wet and consequently fled to the seats above. At Elm Park the roofs kept you dry but they were supported by pillars which obstructed your view. In the Madejski Stadium (with its Transatlantic/Mediterranean design) the priorities were altered; unobstructed views but the occasional danger of a soaking for rows A to K in a full house. Perhaps, with the whole of the 21st century ahead in mind, the stadium was built for global warming and/or summer football!

So, practical stuff apart, how was it going in the new stadium? It was fine, it was different, but it was still a little remote, physically and emotionally, for me. It was like seeing a favourite uncle's garden shed being replaced by an airport lounge. Each is fine in its own right but it's quite a jump from to the other when you're still expecting to see the same thing inside. The Madejski Stadium had its new staff and uniforms and its place outside the town, though we could see week by week the new buildings and roads creeping down to meet it. The scale was bigger and the professionalism was better and the number of people you recognised from week to week was fewer.

One small change symbolised the distance for me. At the Madejski Stadium the touchline is twice as far away as it was at Elm Park. The players are literally out of touch with the fans (a relief for them, maybe). The track that separates the pitch from the seats was still that curious bright red-brown but now it was lightly sprung and synthetic, whereas Elm Park's covered your shoes in real, hard-to-shift dirt.

There were other visual differences that subtly change the experience. Once Wembley was the only stadium where you had no sense of the outside world. Now the Madejski Stadium is one of many where football takes place in a totally self-enclosed visual world. The television cameras never seem to stray far from the pitch so the viewer gets less sense of the crowd and the stadium. The club programme also reflected this visual concentration on the pitch and the players rather than on the fans, the sky, the weather, the outside. Many photos show empty seats right behind the goals, once one of the prime viewing locations. The feel of intensity is now on the pitch rather than in the crowd. The cliché of 'pressure cooker environment' comes to mind but it is not the terraces that are bursting any more.

The new stadium also had an effect on the fans' self-image and, more particularly and importantly, the players. It unequivocally raised the stakes. It made fans, old and new, realise what the club could be: indeed, what the club had to be. An average crowd of below 4,000, which was our average in this division only 7 years ago, would make a mockery of the whole enterprise. This stadium needs 15,000 to begin to make real financial sense and only the top 30 odd clubs get gates like that. At the time it opened, the Madejski Stadium was the biggest and best football ground south of Villa Park and west of Stamford Bridge, that *is* the whole of the south of England, outside London. It was the equal of clubs like Bolton, Coventry and West Bromwich. It was ahead of say Leicester, Ipswich and Southampton, let alone Swindon and Oxford. Rivals have plans to catch us up so our comparative advantage may not last a decade in some cases. Other clubs may simply be unlucky enough never to be able to make the leap forward and, like Aldershot and Marlow, become half-forgotten foes from a different era.

Reading fans were proud of the new stadium and their ambitions for the club were re-kindled. But with it, and with all the new vision talk, came perhaps a greater impatience for success and intolerance of failure. Some of the crowd seemed quicker to criticise the players or more vocal in their criticism but others took pains to shout them down. It felt that though there were more people in, there was less pulling together than in harder times. It may just have been a function of the team and the first season; we shall see.

Other fans' perceptions also played a part. Relegation from Division One and a three mile journey south to a new stadium made us appear no longer 'shit ground, no fans' but 'a moneybags big club'!

In the eyes of peers like Bournemouth and Gillingham, let alone former League Champions like Preston and Burnley, we had set ourselves up to be someone they did not believe we were. And they seemed anxious to prove it in the only way they could, on the field of play. They raised their game at the Madejski.

There was some schizophrenia amongst our own support too. Maybe half our fan base had been following the team for only 5 years and saw Division One as our natural home and a new stadium long overdue, while the other half was still mentally locked in the old Division Three and wondering what we had done to deserve such a place.

The players, the key professionals who worked here, were unequivocally in favour. The new signings cited it as a reason for signing while the old hands said "Obviously it's fantastic". One said Elm Park was like "Going into a little hole. You couldn't do anything there". In the dressing room there was a feeling that the club was now bigger and more serious, that the surroundings were something to live up to. I know what they mean. In my industry I once worked in the equivalent of Highbury and the equivalent of Turf Moor and I noticed a few tiny mental differences. How the 'Highbury' surroundings gave you a little more confidence (if I belong here I must be doing alright), how they made you stretch yourself to live up to them, how they could make you fear failure, fear feeling unworthy, a little more. If this kind of feeling is to be our new home advantage, so be it.

Caskey scores against Preston.

Play off fever

On 20th February, after the draw at Burnley, Preston came as League-leaders to the Madejski Stadium. The Royals had fallen back to 12th and a seeming mid-table conclusion to the season. Murty and Polston were fit and in the team and, though North End were confident, cocky almost, Reading grittily matched them in a goalless first half.

In the second, Howie saved a penalty and turned the game. Caskey floated a free kick beautifully into the corner of the net. Preston equalised late on but the Groundhog was to be killed off. No more home draws for the rest of the season. In the very last minute the Royals were awarded a penalty every bit as dubious as Preston's (i.e.99%) and loanee Thorpe rolled it home. Good performance, great result – and it put Fulham back on top of the table. Three days later the Royals were at Fulham and gave them a game for an hour, taking the lead before falling 1-3, the first away defeat for five months. Parky went off for 10 minutes in the first half while Reading tried and failed to stitch a deep cut in his eyebrow before sending on the sub. Head-bandaged, he was back to score the equaliser at Colchester.

The Archbishop of Canterbury visited the stadium and pronounced himself most impressed. A few days later Macclesfield Town made their first visit to Reading and were beaten comfortably by 1-0. Thorpe was replaced as 'duty' loan player by Mark McKeever of Sheffield Wednesday for the match at Stoke. The Royals survived a few first-half scares before he opened the scoring in the second. He then made three more as Reading ran out 4-0 winners over the demoralised Potters whose promotion hopes were fading as fast as ours were beginning to rise. There is nothing like a big away win to galvanise the spirits of the faithful and thousands travelled to, and hundreds were locked out of, Dean Court, Bournemouth on the Saturday. The Cherries were unbeaten at home all season but Reading defended well and McKeever's second half goal won the match in possibly our best result of the season.

A slightly disappointing crowd of just over 10,000 was at the Madejski Stadium to see the local derby against relegation-threatened Wycombe, now under the new management of former Reading favourite, Lawrie Sanchez. From a Wycombe mistake, McIntyre gave the Royals the lead. McKeever (who after just two away games had been accorded his own song!) did not dominate as expected. Bernal brought down a Wycombe forward as he was about to score and was sent off again (his 8th time for Reading). Carroll put the penalty into the North Stand and Reading re-shuffled, sacrificing Sarr for on loan centre-back Barras in an attempt to hang on.

Murty between injuries.

It wasn't easy but Reading played it well and Caskey headed a second to give Reading some breathing space. Wycombe scored late on but it was not enough to stop the Royals' fourth win on the trot.

The other teams challenging for promotion were all doing well too, so it was vitally important to keep winning matches as the season entered its last 10 games. Reading were 6 points behind Gillingham and still had to play them. Victory there would narrow the gap to three points and the momentum of a successful run would work in our favour. Wigan, further behind, had a lot more games in hand. We had a chance but it would mean picking up 20 points from 10 games, four against clubs also involved in the same race. There was a strange atmosphere at Luton where the home club had just been put into financial receivership. Luton had been a similar sort of club to Reading but its post-war history had been much more successful. However, Luton's benefactor had failed to get new stadium plans off the drawing board and seemed to have abandoned the cause as a consequence of that and subsequent fan protest. Here was an illustration of the fate of two clubs being determined by events, processes and characters all off the pitch. Motivated by their plight the Luton players stormed into the game and took an early lead. Then they missed a penalty, the third consecutive miss Reading had enjoyed. Murty was kicked out of the game and for the rest of the season. Reading pushed them back in the second half and equalised through Tony Barras. He had more chances to win the game but it finished 1-1. Afterwards Tommy Burns said, "That's the benefit of having big, physical players in the squad".

With 9 games to go and the transfer deadline upon us, Burns went shopping again, this time adding five players to the squad for the run-in. Top buy was Sean Evers from Luton for £500,000. He was out with a stomach strain (and subsequently was only to play half a match in the rest of the season). Keith Scott, a traditional, experienced 'barnstorming' centre forward came from Wycombe, Andy McLaren, a winger from Dundee United joined and on loan Tony Barras was signed full-time from York. Alan Maybury, a right back, was also taken on loan, from Leeds. These signings took Burns's outlay to £3 million on 21 players, according to one media source. The spending was a clear expression of intent to use the last 9 games as a springboard to get us from 7th into the play-offs and then on to win the play-offs. Our next opponents were 6th placed Manchester City who, after a bad start, were on a long run which had contained only one defeat. City were by far the biggest and best supported club in the division and had sold enough tickets to fill the South Stand of the Madejski Stadium. It was a case of two ambitious, on-form teams meeting in a packed, modern stadium. It could be a game that set the whole thing alight (not literally!).

"On yer head, Your Grace".   "Archie, Archie".

In the programme John Madejski wrote from Malaysia, "Days like today are the reason we are all captivated by the game of football, and I'm sure the stadium will prove a fitting arena for this afternoon's vital game. The stadium will really come into its own today and we want to see more and more occasions like this on a regular basis."

Because an England World Cup qualifying match was kicking off at 3pm, the Reading game was brought forward to 1pm and supporters were invited to stay behind and watch the England match on the TV sets in the concourses; all very modern. The East and South Stands were completely sold out and there were a fair few City shirts in the home North Stand. Even though it felt like an old style football invasion, at 1pm there were still large gaps in the away end. The roads (or lack of them) had again defeated the traffic and kick off was delayed until 1.30pm, thus thwarting many plans of watching both matches in their entirety. Finally, the crowd of 20,055 settled. It was a new ground record, the largest League crowd anywhere that day and the biggest home League gate since March 1962. Those who had asked why does a Division Two side need a 24,000 seater stadium were almost completely answered.

Of the deadline day signings, all but Evers took part and Reading, despite four new players (including two loanees), settled quickly and played some decent stuff. City were strong in organisation and belief though and did not allow the Royals to penetrate. Both sets of supporters were getting behind their teams and when the game most needed a Reading goal (well I would say that) it got one from City. Barras fouled clumsily on the edge of the area and Terry Cooke's free kick beat Howie's hand and slid into the corner of the net. One down in a game we needed to win, we came out for the second half in a more attacking formation. It was an improvisation too far. The defence was no longer secure. Twice Shaun Goater broke through and the second time he scored. What was looking difficult quickly became impossible as Maybury brought a breaking Paul Dickov down from behind and was sent off. Cooke scored wonkily from the free kick and once more large portions of the Reading crowd upped and left with nearly half an hour to go. This mass early exit was becoming a feature of defeat at the Madejski, the desire to beat the traffic compounded on this day by the desire to see the England game. Announcements made, saying that the concourse TVs would not immediately be switched on for safety reasons, added to the exodus. Debutant Keith Scott pulled one back but this particular game was disappointingly up and the next game at Gillingham became make-or-break.

Record attendance V Manchester City.

Kevin Keegan, manager of Fulham and England at the Madejski.

Post match chilling.

Post match grilling.

End of season report.

It was contentiously rearranged for the Thursday evening before Good Friday, which flattened the sense of occasion. Gillingham scored early from a corner and, with Reading realistically needing a win and nothing else, it was all down to the second half performance. We had a go but, predictably enough, it was Carl Asaba who scored the Gills' second and effectively ended our play-off chances. Thus the Easter Monday match against now run-away-leaders Fulham was somewhat academic.

Nevertheless a crowd of nearly 19,000 turned up on a typical sunny Bank Holiday, the largest crowd ever to see a game kick-off at the advertised time in the Madejski Stadium! Kevin Keegan, part-time Fulham and part-time England manager was warmly welcomed and Reading set about putting in a determined performance against the best team to grace this division for some years. We tried to take them down a peg and the East Stand had something of the spirit of the South Bank that day. On a bobbly pitch, later criticised by Keegan, there were few chances. The recalled Sarr missed the Royals' best by shooting straight at the keeper with the score at 0-0 on 70 minutes. 7 minutes later Fulham nicked a close range winner to decide a game that should have been a draw. But that's what champions do. Even the Reading management now admitted that the play-off dream was over and it would be another season in the Second Division.

Something positive was learned from the two games against Manchester City and Fulham and that was that the crowd would come to the Madejski when the occasion and the opposition merited it. In truth, Reading's late play-off challenge was weak and short-lived but on the back of just half a dozen good results and two classy opponents we had drawn League gates bigger than any seen in a generation at Elm Park and receipts that dwarfed the record there. There was proof of a bigger market for football in Reading and the Thames Valley at, let's say, top of Division Two/Division One level.

After the defeat by Fulham, the players pretty much downed tools for the season. Of the remaining six games four resulted in bad defeats. The side continued to be chopped and changed to the point that another record was set for the number of players used during the season, 44 in all. 16 of these were loanees or had left the club during the season. Only 6 – Caskey, Howie, Parkinson, Brebner, Primus and Casper - made more than 30 League starts. At the end of such a roller-coaster season the players were probably emotionally exhausted and desperate to regroup and start again. The supporters' patience, stirred by greater expectations, was getting very thin.

The penultimate home game against Northampton was played out in front of a flat, passive and increasingly tetchy home support.

The afternoon began on a necessarily dismal note with a minute's silence for the tenth anniversary of the Hillsborough disaster. But for a single mobile phone ringing, it was observed as punctiliously as ever. More than the other disasters, Hillsborough cuts to the quick of fans' own experiences. Most regular match-goers over the age of 25 have seen such situations in the making and can think 'there but for the grace of God go I'. Once it was part of the territory of being a football fan, just like the chance of fatalities in mountaineering or motor sport. I thought back to that minute's silence ten years ago at Elm Park and to all the sadness and pain that was in the game then and how much had now changed. You could not have predicted that ten years later Reading, still virtually in the same position in the League, would be playing in such a stadium as this, 10,000 people standing – for the only time in the match – amid such gleaming modernity and self-conscious safety. Football's capacity for renewal has been astonishing.

The game itself was the archetypal end of season, lower division game of which there had been too many at Elm Park down the years, but I felt a coldness and silence about this one that was unfamiliar. Northampton were duffers, about to go down, but they hung on in a spirited fashion and scrambled a late winner. Just as the previous game against Fulham was what the Madejski Stadium was all about, this debacle was the total opposite, a negation of the facilities. You could have got away with it in Elm Park, it was so bad you'd laugh it off, but football here cost us more in terms of time, money and effort so the failure was utterly apparent and hurtful. The final home game against Millwall was witnessed by the second smallest crowd of the season and, though Reading won 2-0, the day was soured by away fans' attempted pitch invasions and scuffles with the stewards. Some things don't change.

Ultimately Reading's season was one of marking time while the new regime and its players almost completely supplanted the old. The general out-take from supporters was one of disappointment rather than pleasure, remembering the frustrations and cock-ups rather than the brighter moments of the opening day and the good results. High expectations were partly to blame. At home in the League we had won 10, drawn 6 and lost 7 over the season but against the top 10 placed clubs we lost 5 times at home. That, plus the Bristol Rovers thrashing, took the wind out of our sails. The Royals finished their first season at the Madejski Stadium in 11th position in Division Two – and that was not in the plans either!

PART FOUR

THE VIEW AHEAD

A Junior Royal scores at Millwall's New Den. A future Senior in years to come ?

Calling to account

As the Millenium season of 1999/00 draws upon us, what kind of conclusion is there to be drawn on how the move from Elm Park to the Madejski Stadium has affected our football culture?

Anything more than a simplistic verdict is going to be very much of an interim nature. The Madejski Stadium is still evolving as I write. Already the Henley Suite, the Richmond signage, the showroom reception and the smoked glass, corner-windowed Chairman's office (in which he never sat) are gone, in the past. The hotel rising behind the West Stand will be a major, permanent building that will add to the character and probably the match day experience in the decades to come. The surrounding area develops month by month with the onward and upward march of modern blocks.

But, already the simplistic, bottom-line verdict is clear. The world in general (that is people with the slightest knowledge of football) now knows a third thing about Reading Football Club. In addition to Maxwell's failed take-over and our Wembley play-off tragedy, it is that Reading have a great new stadium by the motorway and, therefore, must be a club going places.

Those who have noticed the biggest differences are probably the corporate clientele (and they have been charged accordingly). No longer do club officials have to lead the name-badged and suited elite round the Directors' Car Park and up the Tilehurst slope, past bands of lost away fans, for refreshments on the top floor of the Rendezvous! Now it is all parking permits and carpets, air-conditioning and cuisine, just as in all the other days of an executive existence. It works and it sells.

The boardroom at Elm Park felt like a cramped sea-captain's cabin. The Directors Box abutted rows of the general public and was but a few strides from the pitch invaders. Now the Directors Box boasts padded red seats and bestrides the glass cliff-face of the executive boxes below.

Conditions for away supporters are now far better. Not just a roof on the toilets but also over the seats and under which they make far more noise than ever before. The Madejski Stadium can offer the visiting club 4,500 places with unrestricted views, as good as anything the home fan enjoys though, inside that end, the decoration and the theming of the bars has yet to happen.

The grand reception and exhibition space, 1998 to 1999.

In a Match of the Day magazine poll, the Madejski Stadium was voted the third best ground for away fans in its first season. Satisfying the demand of away fans can be very good business, provided the environment stays trouble-free. A full away end enables Reading to take about £50,000 off supporters of the visiting club.

The disabled, previously lodged in limited space at the front of E Stand, have benefited particularly from the design of the Madejski Stadium which allows easy, staircase-free access and plenty more wheelchair spaces in specially designed, well-sited areas. The media, on the other hand, need to be reasonably fit to get up all the stairs to their elevated third tier station at the top of the West Stand. Unlike Elm Park, it is a discrete area, well away from the public, spacious and offering the most 'Continental' type view of the pitch far below.

Unquestionably, the stadium has created new home supporters, people who would not have considered going to Elm Park, but who see the Madejski Stadium as perfectly acceptable. Some of this is quite understandable. In my subjective opinion there are more older people coming now, probably because of a combination of more and better seats at concessionary rates, more controllable access right up to the ground and a perception of greater safety. Three of my friends have brought mothers/mothers-in-law in their 70s to matches at the Madejski. One was seeing her first Reading game since 1952! There are also far more young children, the Young Royals now have around 1,000 members, and their parents – mums as well as dads.

And, partly subjectively partly based on my professional research into football-watching, there seem to be more people who come just for some entertainment, something to do on a Saturday. Football is such a popular phenomenon at the moment it is difficult to escape it. It's in the adverts, on the main news bulletins, in the betting shops, on the streets in the form of replica kits worn every day, it has its pull-out sections in the newspapers now and the fantasy leagues and there is day-to-day live TV coverage. Once I felt football fans were almost all footballers themselves of some sort. Perhaps they were now too old to play or still too young or didn't have a game on or were injured, whatever, they would just as much want to play themselves and judged things on the pitch from their own playing experiences. The fan as part of football's ladder of life. I don't think that can be true any more. 15 years ago you would talk about football only amongst true believers; now everybody, 'player' or not, seems to have an opinion, everybody wants to partake, to belong in some form. What most people want to belong to is 'the Premiership experience' but it is very difficult to get into most grounds there on a casual basis.

Supporters young...

..and young at heart.

Hotplates at the ready.

The Madejski Stadium, Reading, offers football locally in Premiership-like surroundings and is, for these people, the best chance of participating in live football.

They may well turn into full-blooded Reading fans in time or they may disappear like froth when football, as it inevitably will, loses some of its current popularity. Who knows? But the presence of the uncommitted does subtly alter the atmosphere and occasion. One incident stuck in my mind. During the Manchester City match I saw one middle-aged, casually dressed man return from the half-time refreshments queue in the North Stand 20 minutes in to the second half! We knew he had been there all that time and he had, in effect, missed seeing the game and the season being decided, all so he could get two cups of coffee! Wouldn't a fan have different priorities?

The atmosphere is different now, as it is in virtually all all-seater grounds. Because there is so much more to do, and buy in the concourse, supporters take their seats much closer to kick-off time so there is no sense of the atmosphere building up as it might have done for an hour or so in a terraced ground. Fans are physically further apart from one another because they are sitting not standing, less able to share a joke or comment within the earshot of 6 or 7 others. The singers are interspersed with the non-singers. Sometimes the singers get the non-singers to join in but often it works the other way round. One reason why the away fans sound louder is that only the committed travel. Reading fans sound better away from home too. In the long term we may look back on the 1970s, 1980s and 1990s as the time of great crowd atmosphere. Alex James once remarked of the Elm Park crowd in the 1940s, that he had heard more noise on the greens of a golf course!

The other big factor in generating the atmosphere is, of course, the performance of the team and it is impossible to disentangle the effects of the first season's muted performances from the effect of the new ground. But tight all-seated grounds like the Dell and Loftus Road can generate plenty of atmosphere when fairly full and there is a tendency to forget that Elm Park could be rather leaden at times. For the regular home fans, pride in the new stadium and hope for the club's future is slightly tempered by the loss of atmosphere and the break with the past. For a few I know, the link has been broken and they have taken this moment to opt out of regular match-going commitments.

Overall, the loss of these is far outweighed in numerical terms by the gain of new supporters. Reading's average League crowd, despite relegation and a mid-table season, rose by 16% from 9,676 to 11,262. In identical circumstances at Elm Park crowds might have fallen to 6,500-7,000.

Burger and chips – with moody overtones.

Reading were the fifth best supported club in the Division and a creditable 41st in all four divisions. Yet the scope for improvement was clear from another table which showed the Madejski Stadium as only the 61st fullest stadium on average. Room for plenty more still.

Another league table that Reading are climbing is that of financial turnover, excluding transfer fees (that is how much money goes through the business). It is one way of measuring, particularly in financial terms, how big a club is. In 1996/97 two of our oldest rivals, Millwall and Swindon, had turnovers of £5.1 million and £4.7 million respectively. Reading's turnover was a mere £3.3 million by comparison. After the first season at the Madejski Stadium Reading's turnover is likely to be the biggest of the three at nearly £6 million. Other clubs with a turnover of that size are likely to be Ipswich, Norwich and Stoke. In 1997/98 Reading and Swindon's gates were roughly the same. Last season, Reading's crowds grew by 16% while Swindon's fell by 16%. Swindon are still a division ahead but, if resources are what do count, then this could only be temporary.

There is another key figure that John Madejski points out. Reading, as a business, are still, in the summer of 1999, losing a lot of money. The formula only works when revenue, gates and wages form some sort of equilibrium or when somebody is able to back the discrepancy. The stakes just keep getting bigger. In 1979/80, 20 years ago, Mike Kearney and Neil Webb's time as players, it cost just £1 to get in and watch Reading finish mid-table in this division. Adjusted for inflation that entry money would be £2.63 today, not £12. The club's wage bill has gone up even faster from the equivalent of £600,000 then to over £4 million now, getting on for a seven-fold increase, the price of just staying level in the football boom.

On a more human scale what does the Madejski Stadium mean so far? After the initial dislocations of the opening days it is getting more in touch with fans and fans are getting a sense of familiarity and 'ownership'. It was good, at the end of the season, to see that local league cup finals and the like were played on it as they had been at Elm Park, that it stayed connected to the bottom of football's ladder. It was good to see that it was rewarded with an England under-21 international in September 1999, making a connection to the top of the ladder too. I spent some time there during the close season, getting used to the dimensions, that rather odd sense of the bowl being neither big nor small for a football ground, but just somehow neat. The process of familiarisation and acceptance is well underway for me.

Does it have a soul? Not yet. You can't decree the soul of a place into being; it takes time and events. The Madejski Stadium is yet to see much football emotion and drama.

Families welcome.

Until it does it will have the soul of one of those newly built houses in 'Elm Park' just off the Tilehurst Road. It will come. Its soul will exist in the minds and memories of the fans who witness great things there. To a large extent we bring the soul along in our heads every game. Our reactions are not different from fans of other clubs who have moved grounds recently. Some clubs have treated the past differently from others. Sunderland have embraced their history in the Stadium of Light, Middlesbrough seem to have ignored theirs at the Riverside. Some fans don't care what happened before they started supporting. The history is irrelevant to them. But I feel more do care, more exist mentally partly in the past and partly in the present. You don't support Reading just because of what it is now, today. The past does exist for the fan. You wouldn't make that choice to come to the game if there was not also something in your head that reminded you of the team's achievements and your own enjoyments in watching them. The first thing most supporters will tell you is how long they have been watching their team. The football ground, Elm Park in our case, was the stage that constantly brought to mind those past dramas that justified your fortnightly presence. A year on, without Elm Park, there still seems something missing in the background. We'll get over it. With some success we'll get over it quickly.

Looking to the next century.

Looking to the next century

When Elm Park opened in 1896, professional football was an immature business, less than a decade old. The club's need was for an accessible, enclosed ground where they could take gate money. At the time it was not at all clear that football would emerge as the pre-eminent national sport. Cycling or athletics could have had an equal call and, in its original articles of association, Reading Football Club Limited openly acknowledged its interest in participating in other sports such as these. Football's enduring success as a sport would not have been predicted but the future shape of the game in the form of national leagues and international matches was becoming apparent in 1896.

As we reach the 21st century at the Madejski Stadium, the future shape of the professional game, now a mature business, is quite 'up for grabs'. We are in the midst of a second football revolution. The first came in the 1880s and 1890s when spectating at matches rather than playing yourself became the most common way of taking part in football. That revolution gave rise to professional football in Reading. The second revolution, which has been happening over the past decade, is in the growth of televised football, such that most fans now watch more live football on TV than in person in football grounds. Through almost continuous TV coverage a small number of big city teams have gained wealth, status and popularity at the expense of other clubs.

There has been a football boom going on but the rewards are spread very unevenly and most clubs at Reading's level are losing money. For years people have talked about a fundamental shake-up of League football, inevitably leading to less than 92 full-time professional League clubs. It has not happened but it feels ever closer around the corner. If and when it does, the key issue for Reading is being on the right side of the line, whether that line is drawn under 44 or 68 clubs or whatever number. The Madejski Stadium and the revenue potential it offers is Reading's bid to stay on the right side of that divide, should it happen.

It seems impossible to predict what is going to happen in the game over the next decade. Will the football boom burst? Will football lose its fashionability? Will pay-per-view succeed or fail? Will a formal European midweek Super League happen and seriously reduce the interest in domestic midweek football? Will the game as a whole realise it needs to look after its grass-roots more carefully? There is nothing inevitable about the outcome of any of these issues. In the past, change has been slower to happen than people anticipate and football clubs are more durable than most pundits suppose.

Through the TV camera, darkly.

There is no real point in predictions except for readers in 10 years time to see what was in our minds back in 1999. No single prediction then, but let us envisage the bleak and the cheerful scenarios of how things will work out for Reading Football Club at the Madejski Stadium. If the outcome in 10 years time falls between these two pictures that in itself will be a decent feat of prediction!

What are the possibilities on the darker side? Many new stadia have rejuvenated their clubs, kick-started a new era. Look at Wycombe, St Johnstone, Huddersfield, maybe Middlesbrough and Sunderland to come. In a few cases it has not worked like that. Millwall were one of the earliest of the new era, opening the New Den in 1993, when a return to the top division was much in mind. The corners are open and the two ends and two sides are mirror images of each other; it is not an interesting building. Whilst the stadium generated more revenue, it coincided with a period of decline on the field and financial turmoil off it. Presently the ground is often only a third full. Many fans feel it lacks spirit and atmosphere. The old sense of home advantage has gone and it does not seem to have moved the status and image of the club on. If Reading do not get playing success, or League gates start to fall again, the same possibilities exist for us.

The comparative advantage that Reading now have over rivals clubs through developing the Madejski Stadium may only be temporary. Already many other local rivals, Portsmouth, Southampton, Bournemouth, Oxford, Brentford and Brighton to name but half a dozen, are also planning or engaged in stadium redevelopment. We have perhaps a five year head start.

For the more traditional fan, like myself, the new era threatens to take away some of the things that drew us to becoming fans and addicts in the first place. So many new stands have gone up in such a short space of time, all to the same safety regulations (no seat can be more than 24 seats from an aisle etc) that most football grounds come to look like outlets of the same retail chain. When I began to absorb football in the 1960s and 1970s it was as if every club were its own, individual little country with its own quaintnesses and customs. West Ham and Chelsea always had small programmes, Coventry had pocket-busters and Leeds, top team that they were, had some terrible rag. The grounds could be so different too. Wrexham had the balcony seating of a cinema on stilts behind one goal. At Brighton the East Terrace was massive at one end and down to a few steps at the other. At Northampton I stood on duckboards on a cricket pitch to watch Robin Friday make his debut. All gone now, like those less than flattering club nicknames – the Pensioners, the Moonrakers, the Biscuitmen. In their place clubs are now trying to manufacture individuality through mascots and theme music and rightly so, but it is not the same depth of character.

The West Stand brilliantly lit.

These efforts link with the perceived need to create more 'entertainment'. The crowds in all-seater stadia may be swollen by those who do not or have not played the game at all and see it as a source of leisure entertainment and communal excitement. The modern 'new town' sports of ice-hockey and basketball, sports that in the wider scheme of things don't really matter in this country, have gone down the crowd excitement route. With the relative lack of atmosphere in all-seater stadia you can see how football can be tempted to follow them down this path. Celebratory music gets played after goals, disallowed or not, at some grounds. Indeed, at Middlesbrough, for a while home team corners were greeted with music. In my book, football is a big enough game not to need this and its fans astute enough to know what deserves cheering. I'm with Alan Durban on this, 'If you want entertainment, go to a circus'. Unlike the circus, sport does not offer guarantees of entertainment. But when something spontaneous, surprising or dramatic happens in sport it stays in your mind for a long time. Unlike anything you see at the circus. If football presents itself to its audiences old and new as an exciting Punch and Judy Show it will run the risk of being judged as such, and failing.

So there are concerns about the club over-reaching itself and the game losing touch too fast with its roots and where its loyal supporters have come from. In the Madejski Stadium there is a slightly ghostly, little-frequented concourse at the north end of the Upper West Stand where the crowds have not yet reached and the bars have not been fitted out. It must not spread. It needs colonising by happy fans.

On the cheerful side, the stadium has great supporter appeal and seems capable of sustaining crowds of 15,000 in Division One. Something like two million people live within 25 miles of the stadium, that is, or should be, less than an hour's drive away. The area is known to be growing in population and prosperity while other parts of the country, particularly in the North, are predicted to decline. We are not faced with any noticeably stronger local football rivals. Financially, the stadium complex has got off to a good start in generating incremental revenue. On paper there is no huge reason why we should not replace, say, Southampton in the Premiership in a few years. Clubs like Ipswich, Norwich and QPR have all had Division Three South backgrounds and decent periods of success in the top division. If some mighty football dictator were to come along today and allocate places in the top two divisions on the basis of resources, stadium, crowd potential and Youth Academy status we would very probably get one. But not long ago that would have been out of the question.

If things work out, the Madejski Stadium, with its motorway presence, will act as a landmark for the prosperous, modern city of Reading.

The stadium will become a focal point of the developing area, accessible by public transport and the Park'n'Ride schemes. Around it the mountains of mud and fields of scrub will be replaced by hills of green and offices that gleam. The ornamental waters of the Prudential Business Park will shimmer through tree-lined avenues. The hotel and conference centre will become important, well-known venues in their own right. The city and its business and its waterside leisure facilities will reach right down to the windscreens of the travellers along the motorway.

As with all new buildings the stadium itself will be softened by time. Internally it will be decorated more sympathetically, perhaps in part by fans themselves or local community groups making their mark. Supporters will develop their own names for its places: the 'Mad House' seems to be the current favourite. The unused spaces within the stadium surrounds may be filled in and used for a fans' bar or a family eating area or a football museum. The supporters' Wall of Fame will be filled. Outside more parking spaces may be offered and the practice pitches built nearby. Inside a well-funded team buoyed by the feeling of playing in leading edge facilities may bring about the greatest era in the club's long history.

One day, perhaps, there will be tailgating parties in the car park, American-style, before the match. And, meanwhile, three miles away, some of the old West Reading regulars may be finishing their half-litres in the Foresters, before walking down to Reading West Station and catching a football special train to the newly-opened stop at Green Park, a short walk from the Madejski Stadium. Smart card season ticket in hand and all ready for the afternoon's Premiership fixture in front of a capacity 24,000. Probably against Bournemouth!

On Saturday afternoon of July 24th 1999, the new residents of 'Elm Park' were cleaning their cars and mowing their lawns where, once, thousands of fans clicked their way through the Town End turnstiles. Meanwhile, the Madejski Stadium was formally opened before a friendly match against Newcastle United. In front of a sun-baked crowd of nearly 17,000 John Madejski led out the Reading team to the sound of 2001: A Space Odyssey. A new football century dawns.

Have a good journey.

A.B. Chaudhry
Aaron Prince
Adam Lloyd
Adrian Willmott
Alan Burgess
Alan Hankin
Alan Harris
Alan James Smith
Alan Sedunary
Alan West
Alison Kingston
Alison matthews
Alistair Dowlman
Allen Thompson
Amy Scicluna
Andrew Cove
Andrew Gibbons
Andrew Wilson
Andy Charman
Andy Foster
Andy Hicks
Andy Jackson
Andy Wellsteed
Annabelle Mundy
Anne Newbery
Annie Dix
Anthony Lennon
Anthony McDonald
Anthony R. Whiffin
Arthur C. Withers
Becky Campbell
Ben Bendell
Benjamin Eedle
Bernard Thompson
Bill Summers
Bill Warwick
Bill Stobie
Bob Rowe
Bob Thornton
Bob Thurston

Bob Warren
Brian H. Chalmers
Brian Ashby
Brian Cradock
Brian M. Caswell
Brian Perris
Brian Shaw
Brian Pickett
Bryan Horsnell
Bryan Morris
Bryan Pearce
C.P. King
Carl Barfield
Catherine Wright
Cecily Platten
Charlie Gregory
Charlotte Bishop
Chris &
Shirley Wilkins
Chris Cleere
Chris Elliot
Chris Metcalfe
Chris Morgan
Chris Rose
Chris Wells
Chris Witcher
Christopher Broadbent
Christopher Brown
Cliff Austin
Clive Priest
Colin F. Elliott
Colin Bishop
Colin Charlton
Colin Cornish
Colin Drury
Colin Jebb
Colin Seymour
Daniel Crighton
Danny Smith
Daron Masters

Darren Clarke
Dave Allen
Dave Goss
Dave Husbands
Dave Peart
Dave Prior
Dave Sargent
David Aldridge
David Berry
David Bowcock
David Clyde
Dawn Greening-Steer
David Jewell
David Knight
David Lee
David Wale
David William Rush
David Willoughby
David Zimmer
Dean Madden
Dennis Herd
Dennis Wiggins
Derek Wells
Donald Wilson
E.J.Denton
Edward Vale
Edwin East
Elaine Beazley
Emma Broomfield
Eric Nelson
Eric Perris
Eric Stoter
Eric Wiggins
Eunan Carr
Faye Willoughby
Fe Sindle
Francis Hudson
Gareth Carter
Garry Griffin
Gary Bourne

Gary Deards
Gary Lovegrove
Gary Needham
Gary Purser
Gavin Willoughby
Geoff Dines
George Jenkins
Gerry McGreevy
Gill Parsons
Glenn Brown
Glenn Harper
Gordon Devonish
Gordon Wale
Graeme Monger
Graham Bedford
Graham Loader
Graham Smith
Haydn Middleton, Alex &
Sarah Middleton
Helen Kean
Helen Woodley
Howard Morgan
Ian Blake
Ian Butler
Ian Clarke
Ian Holder
Ian Maynard
Ian Mills
Ian Webb
Icah Peart

Ian Stuckey
Ivor Hipgrave
Ivor New
Jack Gutteridge
Jake Money
James Avenell
James Bassett
James Saunders
James Stone
James Williams
Jason Lane
Jeff Mockford
Jeff Morgan
Jeremy Parker
Jess Nicholson
Jim Smith
Jo Stuckey
John Allen
John Appleton
John Campbell
John Cattell
John Condon
John Cornish
John Flatt
John Liddiard
John Husbands
John Wickson

John Wilson	Lizzard Wyatt	Michael Bullock	Rachel Maynard	Stephen Rowe
Jonathan Duke-Evans	Jiffy Roberts	Michael Campion	Ray Curry	Steve Bicknell
Jordan Telford	Luke Drakeford	Michael Hawkins	Ray Emmans	Steve Cook
Julia Gibson	L & M Faulkner	Michael Tubb	Ray Ilsley	Steve Coupe
Karen Batho	Malc Leary	Mick Foster	Ray Sweeney	Steve Duffy
Karz Sheppard	Malcolm Lee	Mike Parlour	Raymond Sawyer	Steve House
Katie Gumbrell	Manny Perez	Mike Start	Rebecca Jo Ann Smith	Steve James
Keefy Folly	Marc Broadhurst	Alison Matthews	Reginald Brooks	Steve Morriss
Keith Devlin	Marc Van De Velde	Nathan Lewis	Renee Edwards	Steve Ross
Keith Machin	Margaret Edmunds	Neil Maskell	Richard Cooper	Steve Tanner
Keith Sturton	Marian Ann Warren	Neil Palmer	Richard Herd	Steven Wiggins
Keith Withers	Mark Bosley	Neil Warwick	Richard House	Stuart Coventry
Ken Kennedy	Mark Carter,	Neill Rees	Richard Wickson	Stuart Knight
Kevin & Helen Girdler	Mark Munson	Nick Bluring	Rob Morris	Stuart Latham
Kevin Brant	Mark Pearce	Nick Gray	Rob Stewart	Stuart Tanswell
Kevin Chalmers	Mark Roberts	Nigel Baudains	Robert Brown	Sybil Ford
Kevin Durbridge	Mark Shrimpton	Nigel Cox	Robert Burgess	Teresa Look
Kevin Goddard	Martin Bishop	Nigel Meek	Robert Schotel-East	Terry Patton
Kevin Maxted	Martin Mullett	Oliver Booth	Robert Stacey	Tim Andrews
Kevin Paul Wood	Martin Overson	Patrick Lewis	Robin Moles	Tim Brightwell
Kevin Stevens	Martin Witt	Patti Hogan	Roger Murphy	Tim Rhodes
Lee Draper	Martyn Rowlands	Paul Appleton	Ron Bishop	Titch Waters
Leon Bonewell	Matthew Charman	Paul Collins	Ross Morris	The Old Tart
Les Chandler	Maxine Fullbrook	Paul Evans	Roy Strudley	The Taylor Family
Leslie Absolom	Melvyn Lovegrove	Paul Hunsdon	Roy Tranter	Tom Witcher
Lewis Williams	Michael Ayerst	Paul L. Whiffin	Ryan Smith	Tony Bromham
Linda Nix	Michael Ball	Paul Scaplehorn	Sean Kearns	Tony Ella
		Paul Stephen Hobbs	Sean Taylor	Tony Mace
		Paul Taylor	Shaun Dainton	Tony Palmer
		Paul West	Shaun Hourston-Wells	Tony Towers
		Paula Martin	Sheila Wallis	Trevor Miles
		Penny Warren	Simon Eedle	Trevor Paul
		Pete Cook	Simon Gerrard	Trevor Smith
		Peter Baxter	Simon Gibbs	Vallois
		Peter Frost	Simon Hutt	Vicci Elliot & Jimmy Alien
		Peter Jones	Simon Mark Lambert	Wally Hawkins
		Peter Kingston	Sophie Scicluna	Will Hasler
		Peter Rich	Stef Fafinski	William Foster
		Peter Richardson	Stephen Mark Sheeham	Zoë Allen
		Phil Muttett	Stephen Raybould	Zoë King

ABOUT THE AUTHORS

ZAC JOSEY is 25 and works as a fully qualified professional free-lance sports photographer, and photo-journalist. His family has always been involved with Reading Football Club since he can remember. His work has frequently appeared in the club programme and also adorns the walls of the Madejski Stadium, as well as appearing nationally. He hopes for the sake of society that football exists for many years to come, especially in the form of Reading FC.

ROGER TITFORD is married with one daughter and works as a director of a market research company. He has followed Reading since the age of 9. He has written extensively about Reading FC, including the acclaimed book, 'More Than A Job?' – with Eamon Dunphy (Further Thought, 1992) and is an established writer on the magazine 'When Saturday Comes'. He looks forward to spending the rest of his life being told that tin doesn't, in fact, rust.